Cape Cod's Highfield & Tanglewood

Cape Cod's Highfield & Tanglewood

A Tale of Two Cottages

Kathleen Brunelle

Published by The History Press
Charleston, SC 29403
www.historypress.net

Front cover: Images of Highfield and Tanglewood. *Courtesy of Mike Crew.*
Back cover: Highfield, 1960s. *Courtesy of Elizabeth Totten Looney, from the collection of Historic Highfield, Inc.* The Beebes and friends at Tanglewood. *Courtesy of the Massachusetts Historical Society.*

First published 2012

Manufactured in the United States

ISBN 978.1.60949.791.0

Library of Congress CIP data applied for.

Notice: The information in this book is true and complete to the best of our knowledge. It is offered without guarantee on the part of the author or The History Press. The author and The History Press disclaim all liability in connection with the use of this book.

To my grandparents, George and Charlotte McCarthy, who came to the hill in 1960 to care for Highfield and Tanglewood.

And to my new daughter, Mariel, may she grow to love the Cape as much as her mother.

Contents

ACKNOWLEDGEMENTS

I would like to thank the following people without whom this book would not have been possible. I would like to thank my husband, Robert, for his support through the writing process and my son, Baylen, for his never-ending patience, kindness and understanding. I would also like to thank Barbara Milligan, the director at Highfield Hall, for allowing me to access the archives and for answering my many emails; Janet Totten, for always making time and a place for me to research; Bill Hough, the editor of the *Falmouth Enterprise*, for opening up the archives, allowing me to use material, answering my emails and treating me like family; John Hough, for his beautiful memories of the hill and my grandparents; Bob Haslun, for taking the time to answer my many questions; Mary Sicchio of the Falmouth Historical Society for allowing me to use the Reverend Smythe letters; the Massachusetts Historical Society; Harvard University Archives; Hal Morgan for the beautiful photograph; the Rentz family for sharing their memories; Fred Wallace for sharing his research on Charles Philip Beebe; Richard Noble, the school historian at St. Mark's, for the information on Arthur Appleton Beebe; the *Frederick News Post* for allowing me to use photographs and information; Susan Shephard for her wonderful interview and resources; Maximilian Ferro for allowing me to use his report and for responding to my questions; Isa Schaff, the historian at the Noble and Greenough School, for finding the fabulous old photo of Charles P. Beebe; the Stanford University Archives Staff for sending documents so quickly and for allowing me to use materials in this book; Joan Hester, for her tip on old photographs; Mike Crew, for allowing me to use his great old photos of Falmouth; my mother, my Aunt Kathy and my Aunt Barbara for sharing their stories and photographs from their days at Highfield; and Megan Hamilton McKeon for listening to my endless research and providing support for this project.

I would especially like to thank the TerHeun family. They have been so generous, and they have gone out of their way to share personal and detailed stories. I truly could not have completed this book without the help of Elizabeth "Totten" Looney and Pat TerHeun. Thank you for the emails, phone conversations and support!

Introduction

When I was a young girl growing up on Cape Cod in the 1980s, my family would take trips to Rhode Island to visit my aunt and uncle. I remember examining the books encased within my aunt Kathy's off-white bookshelves. Situated on either side of the back window in her living room, the shelves held an array of books and picture frames. Among the histories and photo albums sat a green hardcover book with gold lettering and an odd title: *Ring Around the Punch Bowl*. I envisioned a crystal bowl filled with strawberries and ginger ale. I never did understand the reference to a ring, other than the fact that every time I looked at the title my mind replayed the childhood rhyme "Ring Around the Rosy" over and over in my head.

While I did not dare disturb the green book with the fancy gold lettering, I often wondered what information lay hidden within its pages. Little did I know that its subject was the same subject I had often heard spoken of by my family: Highfield. My mother moved to Falmouth in the fall of 1960 when she was just five years old. For nearly a decade, she and her family lived "on the hill," as we say, in a house situated next to both the Highfield and Tanglewood mansions built there the century before.

My childhood was full of stories of the Highfield Theater, stories of sleepovers at the palatial and mysterious Highfield Hall and stories of treks through the woods to the deep pond that I eventually came to realize was the Punch Bowl alluded to on my aunt's bookshelf. Like most children born in Falmouth, I, too, came to know Highfield and its surrounding buildings.

At the age of five, I began my violin lessons at the conservatory. By middle school, I took curling lessons with my Girl Scout Troop at the Cape Cod Curling Club. By junior high school, I visited the thrift shop that my great-

Punch Bowl. *Photo by author.*

aunt Eleanor ran out of the first floor of Highfield. And by high school, I gathered with friends at the abandoned mansion and talked about my dreams and aspirations under the summer stars.

Perhaps it was the ignorance or self-centeredness of my youth, but I never viewed the Beebe Woods—or Highfield for that matter—as "belonging" to anyone. The area, much like the beaches that surround Falmouth, seemed to belong to all of us. I felt that the woods and buildings had always been there and would remain for my children and their children to explore and enjoy.

There are those in Falmouth who feel a disconnect concerning the Beebe family and their mansions on the hill, but the Beebe Woods and the surrounding buildings do not simply belong to the history of one wealthy Boston family; rather, the land that they preserved, the architecture they

Right: Beebe Woods.
Photo by author.

Below: Highfield carriage.
Courtesy of Mike Crew.

created and the cultural activities they promoted are a part of Falmouth's history—a part of our history.

The purpose of my book is not to rewrite the events covered in *Ring Around the Punchbowl*—the classic text on my aunt's bookshelf—for George Moses wrote a well-researched and enduring classic. My purpose is to expand on some of the research he began, share additional stories and memories and celebrate the tract of land known as the Beebe Woods and the surrounding buildings as historical and significant features of Falmouth's history and Falmouth's story.

I begin with my own story and the day my grandparents first arrived at Highfield Hall.

Chapter 1

Hurricane Season

On a Monday morning in the fall of 1960, my grandparents left New Bedford. George and Charlotte McCarthy packed up their belongings and four of their five children—Barbara, thirteen; Kathleen, eight; Michael, seven; and Charlotte, five—and said goodbye to the whaling city that had welcomed their grandparents from Ireland and the Azores.

As they traveled east past the seafood restaurants and garden statues that lined Route 6, Charlotte looked overhead at the ominous clouds that filled the sky and listened to the steady hum of the rising wind. They had made this trip to Falmouth before, but the sky had been clear and the seas had been quiet. Now, Charlotte, who never learned to drive a car herself, pulled her rosary beads from her purse and clutched them tightly. She intermittently gazed at her children in the back seat and the small raindrops now settling on the windshield. She knew that her husband's mind was elsewhere, and so she tried to stay calm despite her anxiety. She watched him and thought he concentrated on the road, but as George spied the Bourne Bridge in the distance, he was thinking of the promise of a fresh start.

George's sister Eleanor lived in Falmouth with her husband, Jim. Their home was situated far from the ocean; they lived in the woods between the enormous summer mansions—Highfield and Tanglewood—that had once belonged to wealthy Boston families. The present owner, DeWitt TerHeun, was looking for a new caretaker after the previous caretaker, Richard Fairchild, moved to Milton to take a job with the Sears, Roebuck and Company. For George and Charlotte, who struggled financially and worked odd jobs to support their family, the opportunity for steady work and a place to live was ideal.

Nobska Lighthouse. *Photo by author.*

The McCarthys, 1950s. *Author's collection.*

On that same Monday morning in the fall of 1960, another traveler headed toward Falmouth. Hurricane Donna, though she was expected to hit the Cape head on and veered at the last moment, still made quite an impact as the day progressed. By the time George and Charlotte crossed the Bourne Bridge, the first winds and rains were making themselves known, and Charlotte watched the water below nervously. The seas rose from three to four feet above normal, as the storm came in on a rising tide. The windswept waves blanketed the canal as the McCarthys entered the rotary and continued down MacArthur Boulevard toward their destination.

Meanwhile, the weather tower at Nobska Lighthouse in Falmouth shook under Donna's pressure. By 5:30 that evening, the fifty-foot steel frame tower toppled under the weight of Donna's ninety- to one-hundred-mile-per-hour winds. As the McCarthys made their way down Route 28, the children counted the fallen tree limbs and repeatedly wiped the rain-fogged windows. By the time they turned up Depot Avenue, driving was more than hazardous and Charlotte clung to her rosary. They passed the town newspaper building and headed toward the train station. There, just before the tracks, was Eleanor and Jim's office. Eleanor took them over the tracks

Highfield, 1960s. *Courtesy of Elizabeth "Totten" Looney, from the collection of Historic Highfield Inc.*

and up a winding hill. At the top, Charlotte looked to her left, and there stood Highfield, just as promising and majestic as ever, despite the hurricane.

The mansion looked more like a southern plantation than a Cape Cod summer cottage. Large pillars flanked the front of the white façade, and Charlotte counted two of the many chimneys as they drove past the porch. Beyond the circular drive, she could see the remnants of a garden—once a glorious sunken garden—now just a gathering of growth and weeds. A greenhouse sat opposite the garden. She looked forward to clearing and planting the forgotten patch of land. Just beyond, she could see a small theater.

Leaving Highfield behind, they turned down the circle and headed about a quarter of a mile to their left to another mansion, Tanglewood, which was situated closer to the small caretaker's house in which they would be staying. The home had a very different style and appeared larger than its sister mansion, with numerous porches and dormitories. Eleanor told them that the mansion housed Oberlin College's Gilbert and Sullivan Players for the summer. The orchestra rehearsed in the large barn, also situated on the circle. In addition to students, the enormous barn also held antiques and other old items. At the end of the circle, Eleanor showed them another small house where college professors stayed. Nearby was the old water tower

The Sunken Garden with theater in background. *Photo by author.*

Tanglewood. *Courtesy of Mike Crew.*

built by the Beebes—by the time my grandparents arrived, the tower was abandoned, except for the occasional bats; it later succumbed to fire.

It did not take long for Barbara and her siblings to explore the area. While there were certainly many buildings, it was the woods that really excited the children. Barbara found a winding road into the forest. Thick with brush, as she recalls, it was very difficult to travel; however, she, Kathleen, Michael and Charlotte discovered a large pond about a mile or so down the path. Like so many before them, they were drawn to the deep pond known as the Punch Bowl. They traveled there so often that they made their own trail.

Meanwhile, George and Charlotte settled into their roles as caretakers. One of their first actions was to clear away the grass in the sunken garden. Charlotte spent many hours growing flowers from seed. John Hough, who worked with George and Charlotte while he was a teenager, remembered planting marigolds with her. The daughter of DeWitt TerHeun, Pat TerHeun, also helped to restore the garden. She recalls the experience fondly: "Mrs. McCarthy, who, in between cooking great meals for my parents, sent a bunch of us to dig up the sunken garden. Under her inspired supervision, we soon had a beautiful garden, which provided flowers all summer for the house and bar." An old family story says that after Charlotte had spent much of her time tending to and recreating the garden, some late-night revelers accidentally ran their car into the pit, ruining her months of labor. The next morning, Charlotte was devastated to find the destruction.

John Hough remembers Charlotte as being very quiet, genial and comfortable to be with, and all of the college students liked her and enjoyed talking with her as she prepared their meals at Tanglewood. He remembered that she always wore lipstick and was very friendly. Bob Haslun, co-founder of CLOC (the College Light Opera Company), agreed. He called her, "a gem—a great chef, very friendly and fun to be around. She was a hard worker and got along well with all of us."

While Charlotte cooked, cleaned and tended to the grounds, George performed odd jobs for Mr. TerHeun and bartended at the Highfield Theater. John Hough recalls working for George:

> *George was the caretaker, and he was responsible for running the place. He took care of the grounds, made repairs or saw that they were made, ran errands in the truck—did pretty much everything that needed doing. Summers, he had me and Brian John, a relative of Mr. TerHeun's from Texas, do the manual labor.*
>
> *George wore a frown, or maybe I should say a grave look, that would break up quickly in a broad grin. He had a wonderful, sort of old-fashioned sense of humor. One time the stage manager was trying to talk me into appearing in HMS* Pinafore *in a walk-on part as a marine, which I had no wish to do. I protested that I suffered from stage fright and George, who was looking on, said to the stage manager, "No way he can do it. John gets stage fright when he goes to the movies."*
>
> *He wasn't a big man but I think he was physically strong and able. His manner was deliberate, unhurried. I never saw him excited or visibly agitated. He took things calmly. He never seemed to be in a hurry.*
>
> *He could be stern with me. One time I hung around the box office for an hour or two talking to the college girl who was working there, and George rebuked me for goofing off. He was right to. He thought the word "cop" was disrespectful and wouldn't allow me to use it.*
>
> *He kidded me a lot, in an affectionate and truly witty way, and I welcomed it.*
>
> *I remember one other line, which I have used myself down the years—old fashioned cornball humor—which George said when someone—I don't remember who—was saying he was afraid of flying. George agreed. "Good old terra firma," he said. "The more firma, the less terra." He had a million of them, as Jimmy Durante used to say.*

Elizabeth "Totten" Looney, the niece of DeWitt TerHeun also remembers working at the bar at the Highfield theater:

> *When* [George] *came…I was old enough to drive and just went to EEC Swift for limes and other things for drinks like I had done in seasons before. However, I bought the stuff in a jar as one would for a home bar. I believe he was a little hesitant to tell me this since I was the boss's niece, so he was very diplomatic as he spoke. I needed to buy whole limes, lemons and other things for drinks that way and not in the expensive jars. Later, shopping, I realized the difference in prices, and did a much better job of getting what he needed.*

George and Charlotte spent many years at Highfield and Tanglewood before they moved their family to Worcester Court in The Heights. George's sister Eleanor and her husband, Jim, remained on the hill and later ran the first floor of Highfield as a thrift shop in the 1980s.

I remember visiting the mansion when I was a child and feeling overwhelmed by its pure majesty and size, even a little frightened. I wondered what lay beyond the first floor. My mother told me stories of the times she and my aunt slept there. Fancy pajamas were laid out on the end of their beds, and a woman brought them ice-cream sundaes before they fell asleep.

With its winding roads, undiscovered paths, deep pond, acres of forest, theaters, students and mansions, the days that my family spent on the hill offered them not only a livelihood but also the solace and magic of the woods that had called the Beebes there a century before.

Chapter 2

Summer Cottages

During the Christmas season each year, just after nightfall, one can meander through a festive string of colored lights in Falmouth's old Village Green. Surrounded by statues of St. Nicholas and Christmas carolers, there is a sense of tranquility that is difficult to find in the everyday movement of the streets any other time of year. Looking around, one sees the historic captains' houses surrounding the green, majestic and peaceful in the still night air. During some seasons, a fresh coat of snow blankets the main street and the row of soft and blurry lights that lead the way into town.

The quaint allure of Falmouth, during any season, lies in the fact that little has changed there in over a century. Certainly, the winter population and the daytime traffic have increased, even in the past decade, but on certain nights sitting in that old Village Green, one can easily imagine the early days of our town when it was still a quiet fishing village indebted to the sea. In a 1926 edition of the *Falmouth Enterprise*, a writer described the early days of Falmouth:

> *Those were the days when the fire buckets still hung in the front halls of the village houses, when there were no street lights and each wanderer at night carried his own lantern, when the sidewalks were paths by the side of the village main road, when the days were soft and balmy, and the nights quiet and restful, and the village traditions ran close to the memories of whaling days whose captains were still with us and the language of the street and the store followed the language of the sea and the ship.*

In the early days of the late nineteenth century, the first summer tourists—wealthy merchants and businessmen—traded Boston's heat

The Village Green, Falmouth. *Courtesy of Mike Crew.*

The Dude Train. *Courtesy of Mike Crew.*

for Falmouth's welcoming surf. The call of the ocean tugged at men like Joseph Story Fay and James Madison Beebe who spent their days enmeshed in the bustle and business of Boston and other cities. The journey to Falmouth was certainly arduous and cumbersome at that

Main Street, Falmouth. *Courtesy of Mike Crew.*

time, but apparently well worth the ride. While Falmouth's salty residents weren't initially too pleased with the pageantry of these early summer settlers, they eventually came to embrace the advantages of a new and lucrative industry. Indeed tourism began to flourish, and much of the public land we enjoy today from Goodwill Park to the Beebe Woods can be traced back to these wealthy men.

Unfortunately for James Madison Beebe, he did not live very long after he purchased Vineyard Lodge on Shore Street. In the three summers he spent in Falmouth, however, he purchased various tracts of land and instilled a love of the seaside village in his children. Not only did Beebe purchase ocean property, but he also bought over one hundred acres of woodlands. In his book *Ring Around the Punchbowl*, George Moses writes, "He lifted his eyes up unto the hills above town and there, evidently because he desired wood to burn, as did almost everyone at that time, he acquired a small piece of what was to become The Beebe Woods." The following year, in 1873, Beebe purchased over ninety additional acres. After his death, his sons looked to those same woods but for different purposes.

In 1876, oldest son, Pierson, chose the hill as the spot to build Highfield Hall. His brother Frank and sister Emily lived with him in his elegant English manor house. Brother James Arthur Beebe, apparently influenced by Highfield, began the construction of his own home, Tanglewood, the following year. While their father had favored the ocean, most of his sons

Highfield Hall. *Courtesy of Mike Crew.*

Highfield Hall, 1899. *The* Boston Daily Globe.

and daughters were drawn to the woods, and we are indebted to them for the large tracts of forest that remain in Falmouth to this day.

Much has been written about the Beebes. Many paint the wealthy Boston family as tight-fisted and holier than thou; others view them as benevolent and generous. In his well-researched and marvelously witty book, George Moses recounts the lives of James Madison Beebe and his sons E. Pierson and Frank Beebe, two of the most notable Beebes in Falmouth. But what of the other Beebe children? What role did they play in the development of Falmouth and the preservation of the land on the hill? Let us begin with the girls…

Chapter 3

Ladies of the Manor

Life was not often fair for women in the nineteenth century—not even for the wealthy ones. While the Beebe daughters—Emily Brown (born in 1836), Mary Louisa (1837) and Frances Lathrop (1841)—certainly enjoyed easy and luxurious lives, they did not enjoy the same privileges as their brothers. The Beebe sons figure prominently in society pages, books and various legal records. They had the opportunity to attend college and create their own wills. These records tell us about the friends they made, the clubs with which they were involved and the charities that were important to them, among other things. Such documents provide great insight into their characters. Since most women of the time were not afforded those same opportunities, the Beebe daughters are more elusive. Unmarried women like Emily and Mary, even though they had personal wealth, did not leave wills. Instead, their brothers took over their estates. Their educational opportunities were very different from their brothers. Therefore, we must rely on other documents to piece together the lives of the Beebe women.

If the Beebe sons were known as lords of the manor, then their sisters would be ladies of the manor—literally. In the 1870 census, when the Beebe girls were old enough to have jobs of their own, James Madison reported that his daughters had "no occupation" and that his wife "kept house." As women of wealth, they did not work. In the 1880 census, however, taken after Mr. Beebe's death, his wife, Esther, reports the occupation of each daughter as "lady" and each son as "gentleman." She also cites her own occupation as "lady." Perhaps this says more about the difference between James and Esther Beebe than it does about their children.

Beebe Esther B	W F 69		\	Lady
—— Emily B	W F 42	Daughter	\	Lady
—— Mary L	W F 40	Daughter	\	Lady
—— Edward P	W M 34	Son	\	Gentleman
—— Frank H	W M 26	Son	\	Gentleman

1880 Massachusetts Census.

James Madison Beebe came from humble beginnings, and he never seemed to have forgotten that fact. His industrious and honorable character was described in the *New England Genealogical and Social Register*:

> *In contemplating the successful business career of Mr. Beebe, we find personal qualities which well fitted him for his chosen occupation. Under a kind Providence, his success, as a merchant, was the result of a combination of characteristics, physical, mental and moral. In his boyhood, and as a young man, we have reason to believe that principles were formed which contributed to his success. In the morning the seed was sown; a most important guide to be followed by those entering upon the activities of life. Persevering industry, prudence in entering upon, and faithfulness in fulfilling his engagements, patience and promptness in dealing with his customers, were among the characteristics of Mr. Beebe. These, supplemented by good health, and regular habits; a sound mind in a vigorous body; enabled him to do an amount of work accomplished by comparatively few of his compeers.*

It seems that Mr. Beebe's only concern about his daughters' wealth and social standing was that they not be taken advantage of by prospective husbands. According to George Moses, Beebe stipulated in his will that his daughters' inheritances were to be "free from the control, interference or debts of any future husband." As Emily and Mary never married and Frances outlived her husband, Mr. Beebe needn't have worried.

The Beebe daughters filled their days with various activities. Though they were accustomed to servants, each girl was responsible for making her own bed. The girls rotated housekeeping chores on a weekly basis and ran daily errands to the butcher and baker. They also helped with ironing, sewing and fetching tea.

They were given quite a bit of freedom, especially during the summer months, to spend time away from home with their friends. During such outings, they enjoyed walking on the beach in Lynn, reading in the forest, going out for rides (apparently Mrs. Beebe was always begging one of her children to accompany her to various places in and around Boston), eating ice cream and listening to music. They also partook in sailing, rowing, bowling, shopping and playing checkers. The girls and the boys needed to be home in the early evening, even in the summer, unless they were out with their parents.

The Beebe girls were well educated. In addition to attending classes, they spent good portions of their days writing letters and reading. They read upwards of fifteen to twenty books per month, plus various sermons, and wrote at least one letter every day. The girls seemed to enjoy classic and contemporary authors, including Tennyson and Dickens. They preferred challenging reads and discussed books with one another and with their friends. They all read and enjoyed *Jane Eyre*, even Mrs. Beebe!

Mrs. James Madison Beebe. *Courtesy of Department of Special Collections and University Archives. Stanford University Libraries.*

Emily Brown Beebe. *Courtesy of Department of Special Collections and University Archives. Stanford University Libraries.*

Oldest daughter Emily lived longer than her two sisters. She was, therefore, better known in Falmouth and in Boston. She died just short of her eightieth birthday after breaking her leg.

Emily was known to her family as Emma. According to Moses, she "conversed intelligently on many subjects" and people found her to be "very interesting." In addition, she was an expert rider. Moses wrote that she "ventured anywhere and everywhere on horseback." Fannie wrote that her sister was also a gifted piano player, saying, "I had such a delicious time in bed tonight listening to Emma's playing on the piano. She played a great many airs and all had their associations and I could really say I passed over in that little time some of the happiest periods of my life—thoughts of others…crowded on my mind and heart and filled me with delight."

Emily, like her sisters, loved fancy hats, and also like the rest of her siblings, she enjoyed travel and was devoted to the church. She lived the bulk of her life with her brothers, Pierson and Frank. As she was the oldest child and

Frank and Emily Beebe.
Courtesy of Department of Special Collections and University Archives. Stanford University Libraries.

Frank was the youngest, there was almost twenty years between them. Still, they lived together pleasantly enough, and Emily organized many dinners and musicals at both the Highfield and Beacon Street residences. A typical night on Beacon Street took place during the Christmas season of 1898 and was covered by the *Boston Daily Globe.* The article stated, "Miss Emily Beebe of Beacon Street, with her brother, Mr. Pierson Beebe, gave a dinner last week, when among the guests were Miss Marion Mason, in gray and silver…Miss Beebe was in a red silk gown, with black chenille dotted lace over it, and diamonds in her corsage."

Not only did Emily live with her brothers, she also enjoyed traveling with them as well. She and Frank traveled together often. The society pages recorded not only her trips in and out of the country but also her whereabouts when she was in Europe. For example, in July 1894, newspapers announced, "Miss

30 Beacon Street. *Courtesy of Bonnie Russell, from the collection of Historic Highfield, Inc.*

Emily Beebe of Beacon Street has left Paris for Brussels." She spent extensive time in England and France, and she wintered more than once in Cairo.

No doubt through her travels and dinner parties, Emily met many interesting people like herself. And though she never married, one can't help but imagine that she must have fallen in love at least once during her eighty years. Though she appears a bit matronly compared with her stylish younger sisters, she had handsome features and held the promise of wealth.

At five feet four inches tall, Emily had light brown hair, hazel eyes and a pale complexion. Her face appeared full and therefore youthful. No doubt her appearance, intelligence and wealth made an impression on many of the men she met throughout her life.

One of those men, Norwegian explorer and ethnographer Carl Lumholtz, certainly treasured Emily. During his travels in Sonora, Mexico, he not only thought of her but he also honored her. In his book *New Trails in Mexico*, Lumholtz describes the area called "Many Pools" by the natives.

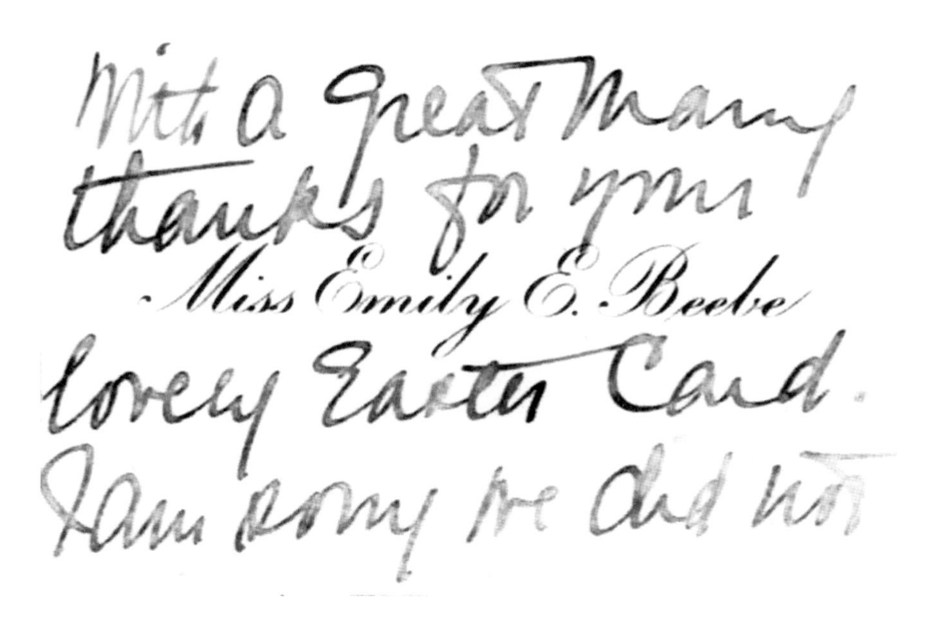
With a great many
thanks for your
Miss Emily E. Beebe
lovely Easter Card.
I am sorry we did not

Letter from Emily Brown Beebe. *Courtesy of the Falmouth Historical Society.*

"The Pagado call the locality 'Many Pools,' and I named it as 'Tinajas de Emilia' for my friend, Miss Emily Beebe of Boston. In a country where water is so rare, travelers hail with delight at the sight of such picturesque reservoirs." Apparently he felt delight at the picturesque sight of Emily Beebe as well.

Mary Louisa Beebe, who was one year younger than her sister Emily, died when she was only forty-five years old from cancer of the peritoneum. A rare form of cancer, even today, it begins in the tissue lining the abdomen. Symptoms usually only occur after the disease has progressed, so the cancer is not diagnosed until its advanced stage by which time it has already spread throughout the body. Well over one hundred years after Mary's death, the survival rate for this particular cancer is still low. Chances are that Mary did not even know she was ill until she was already very close to death.

Due to her short life and the fact that she never married, we know the least about Mary Louisa. According to her passport application, Mary was five foot three inches tall with dark brown hair, dark brown eyes and a dark complexion. Her chin was pointed, and her nose was straight. Whoever filled out the application, whether it was Mary or someone in the office, started to write "medium" to describe the size of Mary's mouth but crossed it out and opted for "large."

Mary Louisa Beebe. *Courtesy of Department of Special Collections and University Archives. Stanford University Libraries.*

Photographs indicate a petite woman with a peaceful yet intense look. Her perfectly coiffed hair and elegant attire betray a friendly and warm expression. Despite the austere setup of the portraits, Mary appears relaxed. Her calm and welcoming manner seeps through the celluloid, as if despite her wealth and family, she is perfectly approachable.

From census records, we know that Mary lived her entire life with her parents and that she spent summers at their Falmouth cottage, Vineyard Lodge. According to George Moses, she was interested in arboriculture and responsible for planting many trees around Falmouth, including those surrounding the village green. He describes her as "artistically inclined," for she painted and placed signs throughout Beebe Woods, including the Punch Bowl sign. Highfield was built about five years before Mary's death, and she spent a lot of time there and at Tanglewood.

She also had the opportunity to travel extensively, first with her parents and then with her brothers and sisters. The photographs of these travels indicate their close bond and lighthearted attitude. One picture, taken on the Isle of Wight, in which Mary appears with Emily, Frank and J. Arthur, is signed, "The Bouchurch Quartet." In other photographs, Mary and her siblings don Egyptian garb.

As a child, Mary enjoyed planting flowers, and her older brother Charles helped her to dig up and take care of gardening beds. She attended school, most probably the Agassiz School for Girls, and she finished her education when she was about nineteen years old. Her sister Fannie wrote, "Today is Mary's last school-day of her whole life. What a terrible idea!" She continues, "There was a party at Kitty Hodges' in Cambridge this evening for all the scholars that leave Professor A's this year. Mary went and I believe enjoyed it very much."

Mary, Frank, Emily and J. Arthur Beebe, Isle of Wight. *Courtesy of Department of Special Collections and University Archives. Stanford University Libraries.*

Though she never married, Mary certainly had suitors. Her sister Fannie wrote of the fate of one of Mary's suitors, Andrew Chadbourne:

> *I never was so surprised in my life as when Mother told me tonight that Andrew Chadbourne was to be taken to the Insane Hospital. She says he has been acting queerly for a long time and doctors and his friends have agreed that his mind is deranged. Won't he be mad? I don't see how they will get him there I'm sure. He had renounced all his family, sent back their letters and is now living on his brother William. They feel dreadfully as I should think they would. Those notes to Mary were signs of unnaturalness. The first one Mother retuned unopened and the second would have probably met the same fate if Charlie had not got hold of it and sent it to her in Pittsfield. It was nothing but silly love poetry quoted. Mary burned it up.*

Mary often went to Boston or on other outings with her sister Emily or her brother Charles. In one funny journal entry, Fannie seems upset with those

Mary Louisa Beebe. *Courtesy of Department of Special Collections and University Archives. Stanford University Libraries.*

three siblings, especially Mary. As a teenager, Fannie seems to dramatize the attitude of her siblings:

> *I must say I just begin to perceive the fruit of Mary's example. Charlie and Emma and all the rest are becoming more and more like her and our family is in a fair way to become one in which the members of it have and pretend to have no interest in each other and show no kindness or thoughtfulness for each other but where each is trying to be first and to domineer and be exclusive and reserved. How Mary obeys the commands of Christ I confess I do not see. I suppose she tries. I only wish she succeeded better. I must do what I can to counteract her bad influence. How astonished anybody would be to read that!*

Despite Fannie's frustration, there can be no doubt that she and her family adored Mary. They often sent her photographs when they went abroad without her. Younger brother Frank signed his to "Mary L. with Frank's love" or "to Mary with love." Pierson did the same. Older brother Charles writes of her in his journals and describes the splendid time they shared in New York. She and Emily vouch for one another on their passport applications.

After her death, the Beebe family honored Mary through various gifts to St. Barnabus Church in Falmouth, including the lectern of solid brass. According to Susan Shephard, a leader in the effort to save Highfield Hall, Mary's siblings also installed a large brass bell in the cove cornice of Highfield Hall in her honor. Her mother commissioned a stained-glass window for Mary at the Church of the Messiah in Boston. The papers reported that the window was "much admired" and that the church was "greatly beautified by this artistic gift." No doubt Mrs. Beebe chose a design to reflect her daughter's own artistic tendencies. It was not until after Mrs. Beebe's death that her daughter's memorial window was placed. The *Boston Transcript* reported:

> *There was much admiration of the beautiful new memorial window, which by bequest of the late Mrs. Esther E. Beebe has been given to The Church of the Messiah, Gainsboro Street, and which was shown yesterday for the first time at the morning service. It is placed in the church in memory of Mrs. Beebe's daughter, Mary Louisa Beebe…Previous to beginning his sermon, the rector, Rev. John McGraw Foster, called the attention of his people to the window and its artistic beauty, and emphasized the marked addition which it makes to the church edifice.*

Mary, like the rest of the Beebes, is buried in the historic Mount Auburn Cemetery outside of Boston. The design of her stone seems to reflect Mary Louisa and the family's sorrow at her loss. A cherub's face is surrounded by a collar of cloud-like swirls and long leaves. There appears to be a tear trickling from the left eye and onto the cheek, as the angel glances downward in sadness. Little did the Beebes know that, like Mary, their sister Fannie was also destined to die young.

Frances Lathrop Beebe was the youngest of the Beebe daughters. Though she died in her forty-eighth year of breast cancer, we know more about her than we do about her sisters. Not only did she marry and produce children of her own, but she also kept an extensive diary in her early years.

When Fannie was sixteen years old, she wrote a daily journal in which she described her family, friends, education and activities. Though she was a teenager and focused more on friends and clothes—as any sixteen-year-old might—her account allows us a glimpse of her personality and her family.

Grave of Mary Louisa Beebe. *Courtesy of Hal Morgan.*

Fannie's reminisces of Frank Beebe are especially amusing since he was only about four years old when she wrote them. The Lord of Highfield himself, the man who was supposedly so strict with his servants, so aloof and pompous in town, is nothing more than an adorable little brother in Fannie's journals. She often watched Frank when her mother was out or if Frank was ill, and she describes playing with him, taking him for walks and putting him to bed. Fannie took him to the woods and made him laugh by "pulling the white leaves off daisies and saying 'rich man, poor man, beggar man, thief—thief!!'" She and Mary also took him to the beach, where he tried to swim "like a swan." Fannie writes, "Mary put him on a board and let him swim and wet him all over and through it all he laughed and screamed with delight." Still learning to speak correctly, he called Nahant "Newhant." He was a good and happy child who behaved "too good for anything" at church, with his parents and with his siblings.

In addition to stories about her family, Fannie wrote about her favorite pastimes, including music and nature. She was particularly fond of the moonlight, and she spent every night sitting by her window and gazing up at the moon. Fannie also enjoyed learning.

In June 1857, Fannie was finishing up her lessons for the year. From her descriptions, we can assume that she attended a school within walking distance of her Beacon Street home in Boston. The girls' school had multiple

Frank Beebe. *Library of Congress.*

Frances Lathrop Beebe. *Courtesy of Department of Special Collections and University Archives. Stanford University Libraries.*

floors and pupils of all ages. Fannie refers to "the little girls upstairs" who had gotten "presents for all the teachers."

The teachers mentioned include Mr. Lothrop, Dr. Folger and Professor Agassiz, all names of Harvard lecturers at that time. In fact, Agassiz's wife,

Elizabeth Cabot Cory Agassiz, helped to establish a school for girls in Boston out of her home on Quincy Street—The Agassiz School for Girls—and used Harvard professors there. Open from 1856 to 1863 and located within walking distance of the Beebe residence, Mary attended the school, and Mrs. Beebe planned to sign Fannie up for the fall semester of 1858. We cannot be sure what school Fannie attended in 1856–57, however, as she does not mention it by name.

The girls seemed to have a rigorous curriculum. Fannie's lessons included reading, spelling, history, mythology and German. During the month of June alone, she read *Barnaby Rudge* by Charles Dickens, *Holy Living* by Jeremy Taylor and Irving's *Life of Washington*. She also read *Dynum Terrace*, a book that she attributed to "Miss Young the authoress of The Heir of Redclyffe," but she did not like the book at all until she got to the end of it. She and her friends also studied Virgil. Even during her summer vacation, Fannie read extensively and worked with some sort of teachers or tutors who examined her and her friends on books and lessons.

Fannie enjoyed letter writing immensely, and she was often hard on her friends if their letters were not as personal or proper. Again, she was a teenager and subject to exaggeration, but the following passages, in which she describes four disappointing letters, are quite humorous.

> *I had* [a letter] *from Annette. It was seven pages long but not what she really thought but merely what any person could have written. She said she did it so that I could write "a good" letter first but I shan't.*
>
> *I got Adie's refusal* [to visit] *and I was so mad I did not know what to do. I wrote back such a horribly fierce letter pretending to be offended.*
>
> *I had my first letter or rather a short note from Lucy this morning and was quite disgusted with it. I had written her six pages of nice jolly stuff as I call it and she dared to send back a little over three pages of note paper which was utterly stupid.*
>
> *I had such a stupid letter from Lucy tonight but still like all her others. She doesn't know how to write good letters at all.*

Fannie seems to be aware of her own petty and stubborn attitude, but she can't help it. She is impatient with the silliness and laziness of her friends.

> *Marianne came home today and came to see me after dinner. We went to walk and then came home to play a game of checkers but Emma…gave her the kitten and I refused to play unless she put it down. She wouldn't so I*

> *carried off the board in a huff and then went back and took the kitten away by force, carried it into the house and appeared no more to Marianne's vision. She left a foolish message with Eddie for me. I daresay I acted foolishly but Marianne is too sickish for anything when she gets hold of a kitten.*

Regardless of the typical teenage squabbles described above, Fannie had many friends at school. They were saddened by the end of the school year and promised to write one another over summer vacation. They exchanged daguerreotypes by which to remember one another. Fannie wrote, "Ida says she wants my daguerreotype and yet she won't give me hers; she says she will when she is a beauty not before, so I refused her mine. Fannie Gray has also been teasing me all day for one so I yielded at last."

The girls would go to the daguerreotype room together to have their pictures taken and exchange them, and Fannie wrote at length about her frustrating experience: "We went and got a pale, miserable thing of me." Intending to get a better one, she went back later that day.

> *Fannie Gray and I waited until 5 minutes of two when, as I tho't I was going then to Swampscott at 2½ , we left without another picture. I went home, found we were to go at 4½ and then went to Fannie's grandmother to get her to let me make a third attempt. This was the most unsuccessful of all for I went and waited until ¼ of 3 and as I knew Fannie was going at 3, I started off not without having had to humble myself into asking a disagreeable boy there to let me go in first and being refused and having that horrid man downstairs offer me his championship to sit immediately. I refused it and carried home the old one expecting to meet Fannie, but I missed her so she got none at all.*

Fannie Gray seems to have been one of Fannie Beebe's best friends, along with Ida, Hattie and Annette. Annette left school before year's end to travel with her family, and Fannie was devastated at the loss. However, she soon focused on Susie Amory and longed to be her friend. She confided to her journal, "O, Susie Amory is too fascinating for anything. I am crazy over her. If she should know me well I sh'd go cracked. She is a perfect beauty and so 'great minded.' She began to fascinate me just in time to console me for Annette's loss." On the last day of school, the girls attended final exercises, exchanged flowers, kisses, tears, promises to write and, of course, daguerreotypes.

Fannie wrote of other family members, including her brothers Arthur, Eddie (Pierson) and Charles. She and Charles, whom she often called

Charlie, rode their horses, attended parties, played music and sang together. When Charles attended functions without Fannie, he came home and filled her in on every last detail. She enjoyed long walks with her brother Arthur and studied Latin with Eddie.

She often shopped with her mother and described the various hats she purchased. She also recalled an embarrassing moment with her mother: "I tried to mend my grey dress and thought I had succeeded at least I made myself very uncomfortable but when I carried it to mother she and Miss Holt and Emma laughed unmercifully at me."

Fannie also described family outings with her father, mother, Charles, Mary, Arthur, Eddie and Emma to ride horses and visit the Lowell Institute. She described parades and eating Washington Pies. She often ran errands for her mother. On one such occasion, she and her friend Lucy were caught in a storm. Fannie pondered the incident in a curious passage:

> *We were on Beacon Mall when a tornado arose and almost blew us off our feet. The dust too whirled around and up terribly. Then the rain came down and we ran home. The shower continued, accompanied by thunder and lightning. One crash in particular startled everybody. I felt for a minute perfectly stunned. It seemed to me for about five seconds as if the world were coming to an end. It is a terrible thing to realize but the impression passed away as soon as the storm.*

Fannie also lingered on more adult themes when she described the farewell sermon of a Dr. W. She apparently liked the man very much and was moved to tears by his words. She even cited his text: Second Corinthians 13:11: "Finally, brethren, farewell. Be perfect, be of good comfort, be of one mind, live in peace; and the God of love and peace shall be with you."

In still another example, during the summer of 1857, Fannie injured her back and confided her deepest worries in her journal:

> *My comfort is that even if it is injured (and I know it is) it is only a part of the body, not of the soul and even if I should die it would not be so bad as to live a hundred years and then die without a hope in Christ. I do not mean to say I have not an instinctive dread of death for I have. It even makes me feel sick to hear anyone describe any injury or pain.*

Like any girl her age, Fannie mentions love (or at least the idea of it). She and her friends squeal with delight as soldiers march by them in a parade.

One of the soldiers "eyed them" and Fannie wrote, "We screamed actually." She talks of receiving bows from F. Asher, Mr. Butler and Wolcott. She would not wed her husband-to-be, however, for another six years.

After she finished her schooling and prior to her marriage, Fannie spent a great deal of time traveling. She spent time with her brothers Charles and Pierson in Europe. In 1862, she joined the Niagara Party on a trip to Canada. American poet Henry Wadsworth Longfellow joined the party, which "left Boston on June 4 and returned on June 16, having completed a journey that took them to Niagara over Albany and Trenton Falls and back by way of Toronto, Kingston, Montreal, and Burlington." Longfellow was married into the wealthy Appleton family, and soon enough both Fannie and J. Arthur would marry into the family as well.

Fannie actually met her husband, George Jenckes Fiske, through her father. Born in Wrentham, Massachusetts, Fiske began working as a clerk for James Madison Beebe around 1848 when Fiske was nineteen years old. He continued in that role for seven years, after which he became a partner until 1865. According to volume 23 of *The New England Historical and Genealogical Register*, "In consequence, partly no doubt, of his close attention to business, his health grew delicate, and bronchial difficulties developed themselves so decidedly that he was obliged to dissolve connections with that firm." He went abroad in hopes of restoring his health.

When he returned in the summer of 1866, he and Fannie were married at St. Paul's Church in Boston on August 16 by the Reverend W.R. Nicholson. They returned to Europe almost immediately, where their two children, George Stanley and Esther Lathrop, were born. Unfortunately, Fiske's health never improved, and he died within two years of his wedding to Fannie. The register describes his outlook: "He had much to attach him to earth, but as he gradually went down to the grave, his peace resembled the quietness of the setting sun. His last words were, 'How good God is! I know that God loves me.'"

Frances buried her husband in Nice, France, where their children were born and where they resided. Her brother Charles had died in Nice only two years before. Ship records indicate that the Beebe family traveled to Europe around the time of Fiske's death, no doubt to help Fannie with her grief and with her two babies.

Eventually, Fannie returned to America with her children. After the death of her father in 1875, she commissioned the building of two homes for her family. The first home, 261 Clarendon in Boston, was designed by Cummings and Sears and built in 1876. Fannie continued to use this home in Boston until her death in 1890. Like her brothers, she also built a home in Falmouth. At about the same time Pierson was clearing land on the hill to build Highfield, Fannie designed her own residence by the water. George Moses writes:

> *In the summer of 1876…Frances Lathrop…had a Shore Street area house originally owned by Mr. Beebe moved to a site on the water some two-tenths of a mile east of the center of the Old Stone Dock. There, combining it with parts of others, she had it remodeled into a summer place of rather uncertain architecture…and named it Waterside.*

Fannie entertained in Boston, but not as lavishly as her siblings. The *Globe* described one such dinner: "Mrs. George J. Fiske of Clarendon Street gave a small dinner Tuesday night. The table decorations of roses and orchids were especially artistic." She did, however, make an exception for her daughter's debut in February 1888:

> *About 100 persons were present last night at the reception given by Mrs. George J. Fiske in honor of her daughter's* [Miss Esther] *introduction into society. The parlors were decorated with flowers and potted plants and the Salem Cadets Band filled the air with witching music. The young debutante looked charming in a very becoming costume of white satin with pearl ornaments. Dancing and supper were some of the diversions participated in by the guests.*

Two years after that party, Fannie died of breast cancer. Her children, both of whom lived with her at the time, retained her properties. They also purchased 65 Commonwealth Avenue in Boston and combined it with the Clarendon Street house where they lived for the next twenty-three years.

Fannie's son, George Stanley Fiske, received three degrees from Harvard University and became an Episcopal minister. He graduated from Harvard the year after his mother's death in 1891. In the Secretary's Report for Harvard, he writes, "I entered the Episcopal Theological School at Cambridge, Massachusetts, in the autumn of 1895, and graduated from it on June 15, 1898. I was made a deacon of the Protestant Episcopal Church on June 5, 1898. In October 1898, I became assistant to the rector of Grace Church at Lawrence, Massachusetts." Eventually, Fiske became the rector of St. Andrew's Episcopal Church in East Boston. He served at many of the funeral masses for Beebe family members, including his cousins Arthur and Emily. After leaving his mother's home on Clarendon Street, Fiske moved to Commonwealth Avenue, where he remained until his death in 1936. He was also devoted to Falmouth and St. Barnabus Church, where the font was given in memory of his mother and where he instituted many needed reforms.

Fannie's daughter, Esther Lathrop, married Gardiner Green Hammond, another Harvard alum, in 1893 (three years after her mother's death). The wedding was covered in all of the Boston papers before the event took place. Sources cited Esther shopping in Boston with her aunt Emily to prepare for the wedding while her fiancé had his farewell bachelor dinner at the Somerset club with twenty-six guests. The *Globe* covered the wedding in its article, "Well-known Boston Society Girl Wedded at Falmouth," part of which appears below:

> *At noon today the marriage of Miss Esther Lathrop Fiske of Boston to Gardiner Greene Hammond took place in St. Barnabas church in the presence of relatives and friends to the number of nearly 200. The bride, who wore a white satin dress with long train, trimmed with lace and orange blossoms, was given away by her brother, George Stanley Fiske. A wedding breakfast and reception followed at the residence of E. Pierson Beebe, uncle of the bride.*

Esther and her husband were noted as "very high standing in society" and "numbered among Boston's '400'." After graduating from Harvard, Gardiner accompanied his brother to California, where they learned the business of grape growing and winemaking. He spent nine years on his vineyard and then, leaving his brother in charge of the business, returned to Boston. He and Esther enjoyed a five-month-long European honeymoon after their wedding; they traveled to Paris, the Austrian Tyrol and London. At first they lived with George at the Clarendon residence. The couple had six children. They, and their children, were painted by such famous artists as Mary Cassatt and John Singer Sargent.

By 1908, the family made frequent trips to Southern California. When Esther and Gardiner separated in 1910, she moved to California permanently. She lived with her children on a large estate called Bonnymede until her death in 1955.

In his article, "The Hammonds and Their Montecito Estate," Michael Redmon, director of research at the Santa Barbara Historical Society, describes Esther as a woman who wanted to teach her children the value of industry and hard work. Though they had wealth, she made sure that her children worked. Her son George even helped to design the *Spirit of St. Louis* with friend Charles Lindbergh. Her children also ran a taxi service for veterans and grew flowers for charity on the Bluebird Ranch.

Esther Lathrop Fiske with baby. *Courtesy of the Massachusetts Historical Society.*

Newspaper reports at the time of Esther's death tell us a lot about the daughter of Fannie Beebe. In 1955. the *Lowell Sun* reported: "Her hobbies included golf, sailing, polo and gardening. On her 73rd birthday, she swam several miles from her estate to Miramar Beach." She was known as a "sportswoman and patron of the arts." Her descendants are the last of the James Madison Beebe line.

The Beebe daughters supported many of the same charities as their brothers. Though, as women, they were not allowed to join most of the institutions they helped to fund, they used their wealth to aid children, animals and the sick. Their memories are cemented within the walls of St. Barnabus, the church they helped to establish on the Village Green. They, too, built in Falmouth, planted in Falmouth and loved Falmouth—the evidence of which lies not only in Beebe Woods but throughout the town.

Chapter 4

The Ghost of Emily Beebe

On a summer evening in the 1960s, decades after the Beebe daughters roamed the halls of Highfield, three young girls prepared for sleep in one of the old Beebe bedrooms. Three single beds lined the wall opposite a nineteenth century fireplace. Each girl sat at the edge of her freshly made bed and awaited an ice cream sundae.

Suddenly, the unmistakable sound of footsteps filled the hall outside their bedroom. The girls eagerly anticipated the arrival of their sundaes but were disappointed when a strange woman in a long brown dress passed by the open doorway. Even more than that, they were confused. Theirs was the last bedroom in the hallway. Beyond it was nothing more than a solid wall. Curious, one of the girls slipped off her bed to investigate. The strange woman was gone. The girls wondered who she was and, more importantly, how she could have possibly disappeared.

As early as the 1950s, visitors and occupants of Highfield shared stories of similar strange encounters within the mansion's walls. While some attributed these anomalies to the spirit of an actress named Fay, rumors also began to circulate that the ghost of Emily Beebe was responsible for the curious experiences.

According to early stories, Emily jumped from a window at Highfield or off of the roof of the theater to her death. Others say that she hanged herself from one of the many large trees that lined the property.

While Emily was indeed the name of the sister who lived at Highfield with Frank and Pierson Beebe and while people have had inexplicable experiences there, Emily Beebe is probably not the source. First of all, she did not commit suicide. She didn't even die at Highfield. According

Tanglewood. *Courtesy of Mike Crew.*

to records, she broke her leg in an accident before her death. In any event, she passed away in Boston at the Beacon Street residence she shared with her brothers. Rather than the young ghostly figure in the stories, Emily, like brothers Pierson and Frank, lived to an advanced age. She was not, however, the only Emily Beebe.

A short walk from Highfield, one finds the ground on which another Beebe mansion once stood. Brother J. Arthur Beebe built Tanglewood shortly after Pierson commissioned Highfield. By 1879, Arthur was ready to bring his growing family to their new summer cottage, including his wife, Emily, and their two children, Arthur Appleton and Emily Esther. If the spirit of an Emily Beebe wanders, she wanders the spot that housed Tanglewood, for despite their wealth and status, the family of J. Arthur Beebe suffered unspeakable tragedy and despair.

Born in 1846, Arthur was the second-to-last child born to James Madison and Esther Elizabeth Beebe. As a boy, he attended the Epes S. Dixwell School in Boston, also known as the private Latin School, located in Boylston Place. In his book *A Late Harvest: Miscellaneous Papers Written Between Eighty and Ninety*, Charles William Eliot describes the curriculum Arthur would have encountered:

Mr. Dixwell was a delightful teacher of Greek and Latin, though his real love was Latin. He always endeavored to illustrate the lesson of the day with objects of art, or with maps or pictures; and in these ways he called his pupils' attention to the real meaning of the text, and often to its elegances and beauties...At that time, the master in each room opened the morning exercises by reading a passage from the Bible and offering prayer...Mr. Dixwell read the Bible simply, reverently, and clearly, and would sometimes make a comment as he read. I have always remembered a comment he made with strong conviction on the first sentence in Genesis: "That," said Mr. Dixwell, "is the most sublime sentence in the English language."

The school served as a preparatory school for Harvard College, and not surprisingly, Arthur entered Harvard in 1862. Arthur was never destined to graduate with his class, however, as ill health forced him to leave at the beginning of his sophomore year. Still, Harvard and the friendships he made there had significant and lasting impact on the young man. He maintained many of these friendships for the remainder of his life, and he willed the majority of his property to the college. Though he went by his middle name, Arthur, when he was with his family, he was simply known as "Beebe" by the Harvard classmates he held so dear.

Upon leaving Harvard in 1863, Arthur began work as a wool merchant in his father's firm. Soon thereafter, he met and married Emily Appleton—a wealthy Boston socialite from the prestigious Appleton family. With his father's substantial fortune, Arthur didn't need to marry a girl of means. He didn't need to marry at all. In fact, brothers Pierson, Frank and Charles never married into other Boston families, even though it was considered the thing to do among the Boston

J. Arthur Beebe. *Courtesy of the Harvard University Library.*

elite. Yet Arthur was a romantic. Fannie recalls that Arthur brought "lovely" girls with him on their various family outings. And so by age twenty-three, Arthur embarked on a new life with his bride.

The young couple was certainly very well suited to one another. They shared a passion for animals, music, theater and entertainment. More importantly, they shared a free-spirited enjoyment of life, family and people in general that really separated them for the other Beebes.

The couple had three children: Arthur Appleton, born in 1872; Emily Esther, born in 1878; and Charles Philip, born in 1884. Arthur loved children, and he and Emily filled their Falmouth and Boston homes with parties and cultural events in which their children took part. The family often appeared in the society pages of Boston newspapers, where every detail of their expensive entertainments was covered, like the following description of their 1892 housewarming party at their residence on Commonwealth Avenue:

> *Mr. and Mrs. Arthur Beebe's housewarming Monday night was one of the events of the season, in which society participated in generous numbers. It was a rare pleasure to see all who accepted Mr. and Mrs. Beebe's invitations to roam over such a perfectly appointed home, built and decorated in the style of the best period of the Renaissance, which was open from the top floor to the drawing rooms and brilliantly lighted. The young people were bidden for Miss Emily Beebe from 7 to 8, when they had a merry frolic and dance and supper. From 10 until past midnight their elders made merry with a costume leap year dance on the splendid polished floor of the hall and parlors. The house is lighted thoroughly by electricity—the pear-shaped bulbs...around the hall being most charming in effect. The alcove under the staircase in the hall was fitted with ferns behind which the orchestra was placed. Norton, who had entire charge of the decorations, made the parlor mantel a line of pink and white orchid bloom, and filled the big library windows with plants in full flower. In the corners of the parlors were tall palms, which set off the red and white tints of the walls. The broad winding staircase, with its carved white balusters and moss green carpets takes one side of the house with its spacious library, while the parlors make the other, the dining room, than which there is not a finer in the Back Bay, being the end room and reaching across both halls and parlors. The whole house is open from the hall to the top, making a full sweep of air and light. Mr. Beebe very wisely moved in just enough furniture for the comfort of his guests, so that nothing superfluous had place. A huge oblong basket of*

yellow jonquils was in the centre of the table. It being a leap year party, Mr. Beebe was the recipient of a number of big bouquets of tulips and other showy flowers tied with broad red and yellow ribbons.

The housewarming was glamorous enough to earn two articles in the *Boston Daily Globe*. A second reporter who attended the gala and described the home as a "palace" commented:

The housewarming given by Mr. and Mrs. J. Arthur Beebe at their new home, 199 Commonwealth Ave, last evening, was an event which will linger long in the memory of Back Bay's swellest society. Mr. and Mrs. Beebe's house was recently completed, and its elegantly yet simply furnished apartments, with its broad halls and staircases were the subject of much admiration. In the early part of the evening Miss Beebe received her young friends and entertained them until 9 o'clock, when an elaborate spread was served, following which the young ladies had a good night. Between 10 and 12 o'clock a leap-year ball was given by the host and hostess and all parts of the house were thrown open to the inspection of friends.

Often, Emily organized events around the charities and causes she and her friends supported, and unlike many in high society who made sure their offspring were out of sight for such events, she included her children in the festivities. Rather than serving as mere spectators, young Arthur and Emily actually took part in their parents' fundraising events. The following write up describes a typical charity event in the Beebe home:

The first children's performance for the Kindergarten of the Blind took place at Mrs. J. Arthur Beebe's yesterday afternoon at 4:30 before a brilliant company. Master Arthur Beebe played The Archer. Miss Emily Beebe performed in "The Pageant" by Christina Rossetti with many other girls.

Emily also made sure that her entertainments were suited for children as well as adults, no doubt in hopes to include and instruct her own children. The program of theatrical performances held at the Commonwealth Avenue home included many for young children, and the house was well suited for performances:

Mrs. Arthur Beebe gave a charming entertainment Tuesday afternoon at her Commonwealth Ave. home. The pretty little play, "Alice in Wonderland,"

> *and the Greek dance, which was given last winter at the same home by a group of young...girls, proved a most attractive programme. The lower part of Mrs. Beebe's house is admirably fitted for any entertainment of this kind. The spacious parlor serves for the stage, and the broad doors opening into the wide hall make it possible for all seated to see perfectly what goes on in the parlor. Then the broad stairway can be utilized...having the effect of an easy balcony at the theatre.*

Tanglewood also served as a venue for summer musicals and fundraising. The following description was typical of a summer event at the J. Arthur Beebe's summer cottage:

> *On Friday, Mrs. Beebe gave a musicale in aid of a charity, when her attractive music room was full of guests. Miss Augot Lunde sang several selections, her Norwegian songs being specially charming, and Mrs. Andrew Robeson recited from different authors, her imitation of children being most true to nature...Mrs. Beebe's musicales are quite the event of the summer at Falmouth, and her house is admirably adapted to large entertainments.*

Like any respectable wealthy family, the J. Arthur Beebes contributed to many charities. Certainly influenced by her mother, Emily Appleton Beebe donated large sums of money to animal welfare. She and husband Arthur shared a love for animals and supported the Massachusetts Society for the Prevention of Cruelty to Animals. In fact, Emily's mother was the co-founder of the organization. After reading an article in a Boston paper by George Thorndike Angell about two horses that were literally ridden to death, she provided the financial backing to start the organization dedicated to the welfare of animals. Within one year, the first anticruelty act was passed in Massachusetts.

Emily Beebe also supported many charities for children. The papers report her involvement with charities for blind children, infant nurseries and hospitals and what was referred to as a hospital that served "colored women and their children." Emily seemed to want to provide a voice for the voiceless—women, children, minorities and animals—through her charity work.

Like his wife, J. Arthur Beebe seemed to continue the charitable pursuits of his parents. Much like his siblings, Arthur loved nature. In 1884, he was elected a life member of the Massachusetts Horticultural Society. Mount Auburn Cemetery, where the Beebe family is buried and famous for its beautiful gardens, was created by the society. Arthur also contributed to hospitals, churches and educational institutions.

J. Arthur Beebe. *Courtesy of the Massachusetts Historical Society.*

In addition to their charitable endeavors, the Beebes shared a love for music and theater. As previously stated, Emily often hosted musicals to raise funds for various charities, and she and her husband frequently attended orchestras and theatrical productions. They tied their love for music with their greatest love—the church. The two personally supported Trinity Church in Boston and the family built St. Barnabus in Falmouth.

Prior to the erection of St. Barnabus, the Beebes attended services at the Falmouth Town Hall. Not only did J. Arthur donate

St. Barnabus, Falmouth. *Courtesy of Mike Crew.*

instruments for the musical portions of the service, but he also sang bass in the choir.

The J. Arthur Beebes lived in many grand residences fitted for lavish entertaining. Before moving to their Commonwealth Avenue home in Boston, they entertained on Beacon Street. In 1891, just over a decade after Tanglewood was built, they spent the summer in Bar Harbor and entertained there extensively. They even considered building on a lot in Bar Harbor in the winter of 1889.

In addition to gilded surroundings and lavish décor, the J. Arthur Beebes offered something else at their grand parties: fun. George Moses recounts, "For years it was the custom for guests at Tanglewood to have their heights and weights recorded for posterity on the stairway as they entered and left the dining room. Scales were kept handy and the figures written on the staircase."

The Beebes also enjoyed traveling. Most of the Beebe family spent significant time in Europe. The J. Arthur Beebes also traveled throughout

The Beebe family at Tanglewood. *Courtesy of the* Falmouth Enterprise.

the United States—often attending entertainments and charities organized by their society friends. Newspaper accounts record their time in Lenox as guests of the many cottagers there. They spent most of their time on the east and west coasts. They often brought their children Arthur and Emily with them. The youngest child, Charles Philip, did not accompany his parents on these trips. He spent most of his time with nannies or with his extended family. The *Boston Daily Globe* reported in December 1905:

> *Mr. and Mrs. J. Arthur Beebe stopped to admire the grandeur of the Grand Canyon of Arizona on their way to California, and then they lingered for a few days at Riverside, where…on either side of the broad avenue are orange groves all the way, and where the electric road which runs through the middle, similar to our Boulevard, is shaded by pepper trees. They are at present at Redlands. Their young son, Philip, is abroad with his uncle, Mr. Frank Beebe, their objective point being Egypt. They will leave after the New Year for…India to spend the next few months.*

One would think that J. Arthur, of all the Beebe sons, led a fulfilling life. He, like his brothers, certainly had wealth yet he seemed to be destined to have more. He found a fitting partner with whom to share his passions and raise a family. According to George Moses, J. Arthur was the "best-liked Beebe." He was kind to people, regardless of their status or wealth, and he relished the chaos of children running about the house. Yet because he had the most, it seems he also had the most to lose.

Putting aside any private family issues there may have been—for outsiders can never fully know the inner dynamics of any family—the public troubles began for the J. Arthur Beebes in the summer of 1893. That July, a Boston paper erroneously reported the death of Frank Beebe, whom it cited as the son of J. Arthur Beebe. Soon the story spread throughout the country. The *New York Tribune* reported:

> *Frank Beebe, a son of J. Arthur Beebe, of Falmouth, of the Boston family of millionaires, was drowned in Buzzard's Bay last night. He was the owner of the new Hanley-built racing catboat Nobska, and while cruising in the bay Saturday and during a high southwest wind a squall struck her off Bial's ledge, on the Pocasset shore, overturning the boat. The skipper, Frank Perry, of Monument Beach, succeeded in swimming ashore after being in the water about four hours.*

Other papers reported that J. Arthur's son Arthur drowned. Still others cited J. Arthur himself as the victim. Though he had a brother by that name, J. Arthur never had a son called Frank. His son, Arthur, was on the water in Buzzard's Bay that day, and he did sail his boat *Nobska*. He took first place in his class during a catboat race at the Sippican Regatta. The breeze that day was indeed described as "squally," and the sea "hubbly" according to the *New Bedford Evening Standard*. Sadly, someone did drown that day.

Henry C. Bellows and his brother Robert had just purchased their sailboat, the *Cat*, and competed in their first race at the same regatta as Arthur Appleton Beebe. The boys had a successful day, for they placed second in their class. During the sail home, however, they were surprised by a squall and eighteen-year-old Henry drowned. The wording of the report is almost identical to the erroneous article concerning the Beebe drowning.

That evening, the *Boston Daily Globe* ran a small statement in response to the earlier reports. Titled "Arthur Beebe Not Drowned," the text read, "The report published in a Boston paper this morning that J. Arthur Beebe of Falmouth was drowned in Buzzard's Bay Saturday is entirely without foundation and the friends of Mr. Beebe are highly indignant." I am reminded of Mark Twain when he responded to reports of his supposed death, "A cousin of mine was seriously ill two or three weeks ago in London, but is well now. The report of my illness grew out of his illness. The report of my death was an exaggeration."

Though the family eluded death during that sea squall on Cape, they could not elude it indefinitely. A mere seven years later, their eldest son would die alone in their palatial residence on Commonwealth Avenue. Only twenty-eight years old at the time and a Harvard Medical School graduate, the handsome and promising young man took his own life. Newspapers jumped on the mystery surrounding his death. The tragedy blanketed papers across the country. The *New York Times* voiced the question on everyone's mind in its article, "Boston Physician a Suicide: Dr. Arthur A. Beebe Said to Have Ended His Life Last Sunday," published in the March 15 edition:

> *The Post this morning says that Dr. Arthur A. Beebe, a member of one of the oldest and most influential Boston families, notice of whose death was given to the Boston papers yesterday, committed suicide at his father's home on Commonwealth Avenue last Sunday. It has been found impossible to reach any member of the family, and Medical Examiner F.W. Draper, who admits that he was called to view the body, in answer to the query, "Did Mr. Beebe shoot himself?" said, "I cannot answer that question." The*

only facts which have been obtained, The Post says, are that Dr. Beebe was seen walking on Commonwealth Avenue Sunday evening. A few hours later his uncle found him dead under circumstances which made it imperative to call the Medical Examiner. All the channels through which information as to the manner of the young man's death might be had have been sent as tightly as possible. Arrangements for the funeral are held in abeyance until his father, J. Arthur Beebe, arrives in this city from California, where he has been with the rest of his family for the past month. Dr. Beebe was a young physician of great promise. He was graduated from Harvard University in the class of '94, and received his degree from the Medical School with the class of '98.

After receiving his medical degree, Arthur completed his residency at Mass General Hospital and was prepared to begin his own practice. Why would a young man end his life after preparing so diligently for his future? There are very few clues from Arthur's life to suggest what prompted him to end it.

As a young child, Arthur often helped his mother by performing for her various charity events. Like his parents, he enjoyed music; he excelled at the piano. As a boy, he attended the Fay School, which is the oldest junior boarding school in the United States and located about twenty-five miles outside Boston. Its motto is "You can if you will." From there, he went to live at St. Mark's School, not far from the Fay School, where he received a classical education that prepared him for college. The family-oriented institution still adheres to its original focus, which is for students to do and be their best. School historian Richard Noble recounts Arthur's experiences at St. Mark's:

Arthur Appleton Beebe matriculated at St. Mark's in September of 1884 at the age of 12, "from Boston, Massachusetts." He entered St. Mark's in the Second Form (8th grade) and like all St. Markers at the time was a boarding student. That first year, he sang treble in the School Choir, which also served as the choir for St. Mark's Episcopal Church in Southborough. He was the second-ranked scholar in his class, and four different times he was recognized "for diligence in study and good behavior"—a monthly honor at St. Mark's achieved by less than 20% of the students enrolled. The following year he was a Third Former (9th grader). He was NOT in the choir that year, and his academic standing slipped out of the top two places (although he was still considered a "scholar"). He was not listed at all for the monthly recognitions in 1885–86. He did come in second in his Form in the annual Declamation (Public Speaking) contest. The record for A.A. Beebe in 1885-86 is somewhat incomplete ,often an indication of periodic absence due to illness, but there is no confirmation of that. In 1886-87 he was a Fourth Former (10th grader). That fall, he won first place in his Form for a schoolwide handwriting competition. On October 3rd, he along with the rest of the School took part in a torchlight procession celebrating the election of alumnus Edward Burnett to Congress. Academically, he did better than the previous year—consistently 3rd or 4th in his class—and in April he was again recognized "for diligence in study and good behavior." In the annual intramural athletic field day, he competed in the 100-yard dash, the running broad jump, and the 3-legged race, but came in no higher than 3rd in any of them. In 1887–88 he was a Fifth Former (11th grader). Academically he ranked third in a junior class of thirteen. He was recognized for "diligence" and "behavior" in May. In that year's athletic field day, he came in 2nd in the standing broad jump (8' 1.5") and came in 3rd in the running broad jump (14'). 1888–89—he was in the Sixth Form (12th grade—Senior Class), in the "A" Division (scholars). He was also appointed one of five Monitors (senior leaders of the School, like Prefects or schoolwide officers). He was the #2 scholar in the senior class and received the Morgan Greek Prize for outstanding achievement in the study of Greek. For all 9 months of the academic year he was honored "for diligence in study and good behavior." He played in the annual intramural tennis tournament, winning in the first round but losing in the second. A.A. Beebe was elected Vice President of the St. Mark's Athletic Association (the President was the Headmaster, William E. Peck) for that year. Beebe also came in third in the quarter-mile run for that year's field day. Interestingly, he seems to have been forever in (friendly) competition/rivalry with his classmate Archibald Read Tisdale of Norwood, MA. Tisdale was always first in almost everything that Beebe was second or third in. Tisdale was also Head Monitor in 1888–89 (equivalent of school President, the leader of the leaders) and took home the School's highest honor (for academic and overall excellence) The Founder's Medal (Beebe was 2nd). The roles were only reversed with the Morgan Greek Prize.

Like his father, Arthur chose to continue his studies at Harvard. Also like his father, he was known to his classmates as "Beebe." He graduated with the class of '94. Three years later, he supplied the following update on his life for Harvard's Second Annual Secretary's Report:

Arthur Appleton Beebe. *Courtesy of the Harvard University Library.*

> *Have studied at Harvard Medical School since September '94. Belong to Bolyston Medical Society, Boston Athletic Association, and Puritan Club. Went to Atlanta in September, '95, with a classmate to see the Exposition. We encountered a temperature of 107 on the way. Took a camera along and got several dozen photographs.*

Arthur met with other medical students on a regular basis to examine cases or learn about medical instruments. As a member of the Boylston Medical Society, he enjoyed the camaraderie of his peers. Fellow member and later president of the society Richard C. Cabot recalled the atmosphere of the club:

> *There was no rival medical club, and everyone considered it a great honor to belong to the Boylston. Everybody smoked during the meetings...The club was dead serious; no singing or entertainment of any kind. The fellows took lots of trouble about their papers...and the discussion was animated...I thought then, as I have ever since, that it was the most intelligent discussion, from the point of view of securing an increase in knowledge among the participants, that I have ever seen in any medical society of any kind. We did not usually have any "visitors," but we generally did have a prepared case, read by one of the undergraduates.*

The Puritan Club of Boston was also associated with Harvard, as the members of this social club were almost exclusively Harvard men. The Boston Athletic Association was founded in 1887 with the purpose to "encourage all manly sports and promote physical culture." The facilities Arthur would have used included a gymnasium, bowling alley, billiard hall, Turkish baths and tennis courts. He would have also had access to a shooting range and a country club. Gentlemen competed in boxing and fencing matches, water polo and other athletics. Arthur was a member of the association when it hosted the first Boston Marathon in 1897. From these descriptions, we can paint a partial picture of how young Arthur spent his time. And though he loved music, medicine and spending time with his friends, his greatest love was sailing.

J. Arthur's brothers Pierson and Frank enjoyed the time they spent in the woods at their Falmouth estate; J. Arthur, however, loved the ocean and often competed in his sailboat, *Pontiac*. In turn, his son Arthur, who also preferred the sea, became an expert yachtsman. While at Harvard, he sailed in many races against Yale. The following blurb appeared in the 1894 edition of *Outing Magazine*: "The Little Cat's Prize was knobbed by a Harvard man, Mr. A.A. Beebe, with the *Nobska* soundly thrashing the Yale aspirant, *Boodler*, that owned by W.H. Emmons." Other records of Arthur's triumphs with the *Nobska* appear in Harvard publications of the time.

Perhaps we can learn the most about Arthur from those with whom he spent the most time—his Harvard friends. The following was written by close friend Sydney Messer Williams, also a member of the class of Harvard '94.

> *Arthur Appleton Beebe...took his degree cum laude regularly with our class, and his MD (among the first ten of the class) at the Harvard medical School...Outside his college courses, in which he stood well, and his medical school work, in which he took the deepest interest, Beebe was especially fond of sailing, and for several years his boat "Nobska" was champion of its class in Buzzard's Bay. His later vacations were largely devoted to cruising. Much of his leisure time was given to music, especially the piano, until press of other work no longer allowed it. Although never taking an active part in college athletics, Beebe was interested in all class and college organizations, and an enthusiastic follower of outdoor sports. He was a man who preferred a few intimate friends to a wide general acquaintance, and those whom he knew best were almost all '94 men, not only during college, but up to the time of his death.*

An even shorter message, and an even more telling one, simply reads:

Friends,
Thus ever and anon a clear life ends.
Beebe is gone.

Arthur's friends were obviously moved by his death, but one can only imagine the grief of J. Arthur who received the news while he was in California vacationing with his wife and daughter. One wonders if Arthur had ever exhibited such behavior before or if he suffered from any sort of depression. One can only imagine what led to his fatal decision. We will never know. According to Moses, rumors circulated in Falmouth about a "taint" in the blood—a hereditary mental illness based on mother Emily's "depressive" personality. Either way, the shock for his father must have been great. He returned home alone to arrange the funeral and say goodbye to his son. The *Boston Daily Globe* reported:

> *The funeral of Dr. Arthur Appleton Beebe took place Monday noon at his father's house...and the service was attended by a large number of friends and relatives. Nearly all of the available space in the drawing rooms and the large reception hall on the first floor was filled with them. The body, resting in a purple cloth casket, which was banked up with flowers, was placed in the rear drawing room. Mrs. Beebe, who is in Southern California with her daughter, Miss Emily Beebe, was prevented by illness from returning to town for the funeral of her son. Mr. Beebe returned at once upon receiving the sad news, and will immediately rejoin his family in California.*

One wonders what "illness" kept Emily Beebe from attending her son's funeral and why her daughter remained in California as well. Perhaps J. Arthur wanted to shield his grieving wife and daughter so they would not have to face the horror of Arthur's passing. Perhaps Emily stayed behind to take care of her mother in her father's absence. Regardless, Arthur Beebe's death marked the beginning of a string of tragedies for the family.

Traveling seemed to aid their healing process. They closed that summer with a trip to Childwood Park among the Adirondacks. J. Arthur traveled to Europe in 1904 with daughter Emily and again in 1905 with extended family. He paid little attention to his property in Falmouth and even planned to spend the summer on Nahant Beach in the Lawrence Cottage on his return from Europe in June 1905. The family's plans were altered, however,

The Beebes and friends at Tanglewood. *Courtesy of the Massachusetts Historical Society.*

by the sudden death of Mrs. Beebe's mother, with whom they would have been staying. Mrs. Beebe's mother had been living in Nahant since at least 1900 and put her occupation as "capitalist" on the 1900 census.

Though Mrs. Beebe's mother lived well into her eighties, Mrs. Beebe would follow her to the grave a mere six years later. J. Arthur, who was so close with his wife, seems to have given up Tanglewood altogether at that point. Gone were the days of lavish and festive entertaining with his wife and children. Though society pages chronicled his visits to musical and theatrical performances with his daughter, life was not the same for J. Arthur.

Again the following year, he and daughter Emily traveled to Europe. Traveling seemed to be a way for the man to soothe his loss. He planned to return to America on the new liner *Titanic* and cabled his intentions to Rector Smythe in Falmouth. George Moses writes:

> *In 1912, while traveling abroad with his daughter, he almost became a victim of one of the tragedies that seem to have, as the old newspaper cliché*

> *goes, stalked his life. That year he wrote a note to Rector Smythe from Nice, news that Mr. Smythe promptly carried to The Enterprise for this Page 1 item: "J. Arthur Beebe and daughter Emily are booked to return from Europe on the new liner, Titanic." Next day came news that the palatial White Star steamer had crashed into an iceberg in the North Atlantic and sunk with the loss of 1,517 lives. There was considerable speculation in the town about the Beebe's fate, but unfortunately they had either missed the boat or were scheduled for a later crossing.*

Though he and Emily returned to America safely, they could not escape their tragic fate so easily. One year later, Emily was having lunch in Boston at the Hotel Touraine with friends. She excused herself, claiming that she felt ill, and asked her companions to send for the doctor. After returning to her room, she locked the door and shot herself in the chest.

Hotel Touraine dining room, 1910. *Courtesy of Tichnor Brothers Incorporated.*

When J. Arthur heard the news, he literally rushed to his daughter's side. In another tragic twist, however, his chauffeur was driving so quickly that he did not see ten-year-old Harry Sombaulski on the road and struck him. The boy died.

Falmouth residents were stunned by the news of Miss Beebe's death. The following appeared in the *Enterprise*: "This community was shocked Tuesday morning when news was received of the sudden death of Miss Emily Beebe, daughter of J. Arthur Beebe, her death having occurred at the Hotel Touraine, Boston, Monday afternoon."

Other newspapers had a field day with Miss Beebe's suicide, as they linked it to her brother's. News, again, traveled throughout the country with titles like "Society Girl Suicide," "Society Girl Imitated her Brother's Little Suicide Stunt" and "Whole Family Goes Gun Route." Some newspapers painted her as a spoiled and selfish society girl who caused the death of an innocent boy when she chose to kill herself. They wrote that she had "her suicidal plan carefully formulated."

This time, Arthur seemed to have been aware that his child was troubled. He wrote to Rector Smythe only the year before on May 14, 1912, "Whether Emily will catch on to Falmouth again, I don't know. She is better, I should say, but ought perhaps to be independent for a time. She wants to go to the North Shore—more invigorating climate." A couple of weeks later, Emily also wrote to Rector Smythe. Her tone seems cheerful enough:

> *Many thanks for your note of welcome, which was a pleasant greeting when we arrived. I am delighted that there is to be a new station at Falmouth. It is certainly much needed, and I hope to see it before long. How lovely the country is at this season. I have never been here in the spring before, and suppose it is just as fine at the Cape.*

She signs the note, "Thanking you again, always sincerely."

After spending time in Bar Harbor, Emily opened the Rodman cottage in the Berkshires, even giving a musical to celebrate July 4, and returned there the following summer. She spent her time traveling and shopping, but Emily was undoubtedly upset.

Within the past decade, she had lost her grandmother, brother and mother—the people to whom she was the closest. She had no family of her own and spent most of her time with her father. Her younger brother, Charles Philip, had already moved to Oregon and never did spend much time with the family.

Her efforts to memorialize her brother Arthur, with whom she was very close, lasted right up until her death. Just months before her own suicide, Emily donated funds to Mass General to secure free beds in memory of her brother "Arthur A. Beebe, M.D." Before Emily died, she was also deciding upon a stained-glass window to memorialize her mother.

According to the various articles about her death, Emily had just arrived in Boston. Apparently J. Arthur was paying close attention to his daughter's mental state. He had already lost one child to suicide, and he hoped that he could help Emily by changing her surroundings. The *Daily Globe* reported:

> *Despondency due to a nervous trouble from which she had suffered for some time is generally accepted as the explanation of the suicide of Miss Emily Esther Beebe, the daughter of wealthy parents at the Hotel Touraine yesterday. It was first announced that death was from poisoning, but a further examination of the body revealed a bullet wound. That a love affair figured in the tragedy was denied by friends of the young woman today. Miss Beebe…the daughter of J. Arthur Beebe of Commonwealth Avenue, had appeared despondent for several days. She went to the hotel from "Foregate," Mrs. Gordon Prince's summer home at West Manchester, which the Beebes are occupying this summer. Usually they go to their own summer estate at Falmouth, but a change was made this season in the hope that if the daughter was taken away from her customary surroundings, her health might be benefitted. During luncheon Miss Beebe was taken ill and asked that her family physician, Dr. C.T. Putnam be called. She then went to her room. When the physician arrived he found the door locked and heard groans. The door was forced with the aid of employees of the hotel and the young woman was found lying on the bed fully dressed.*

According to the papers, a "rigid investigation" followed. Ultimately, the death was found to be caused by a "pistol shot wound of the chest." Emily's mental state was also recorded on her death certificate as "suicidal during temporary insanity." The findings were almost identical to those on her brother's death certificate, which read "suicide by a gunshot wound of the chest."

Again, unless the Beebe children suffered from hereditary depression, one has to wonder what prompted such despair in such a wealthy and connected young woman. In addition to her money, Emily boasted an important genealogy. A member of the Daughters of the American Revolution, she descended from John Warren on her mother's side. Warren was a Harvard graduate who saw action during the revolutionary war at Bunker Hill and in multiple military campaigns. He delivered the first Fourth of July speech in Boston. After the war, he served as a surgeon.

From photographs and paintings of Emily, we know that, like her brother, she was certainly attractive. Her substantial dowry surely only enhanced her prospects, yet she never married. By the time of her death, she was already heading into her late thirties and destined to remain single. Whether her mental condition contributed to this fact is difficult to say. Her parents certainly made every effort to introduce their daughter into Boston society. For some reason, which may or may not have had to do with Emily, the Beebes had to cancel and reschedule her coming out party. Regardless, Emily's parents hosted two events, the first of which was tea. In November 1896, the *Globe* reported:

> *A large affair will be the reception and tea given by Mr. and Mrs. J. Arthur Beebe for their daughter, Miss Emily Beebe, on Tuesday, from 4:30 until 7 at their home...Miss Beebe starts out especially equipped for success and a good time this winter, says an insider. Her mother was one of the Boston Appletons, and their connection is large and blue-blooded. On her father's side, she has two bachelor uncles, Mr. Pierson and Mr. Frank Beebe, Somerset Club men of leisure and wealth, who, with their sister, Miss Emily Beebe, have a handsome establishment on Beacon Hill, and entertain often and well. They are devoted to their brother's children, and will do a great many nice things for their niece.*

That same month, the Beebes sent out cards to announce their daughter's coming out ball to take place in January. The *Globe* predicted that the event would "call out all the buds of the season." The event took place just after the New Year to coincide with Emily's nineteenth birthday. Her debut made the Boston papers:

> *The most brilliant society event of the season thus far was the dance given by Mr. and Mrs. J. Arthur Beebe at their superb double house on Commonwealth Avenue Thursday evening, to introduce their daughter, Miss Emily Beebe. All the rooms on the first floor open into each other, making an ideal hall for dancing, the whole interior being perhaps as beautiful as any house in the city. The orchestra was placed in one of the drawing rooms behind a screen of palms...Mrs. Beebe was handsomely dressed in Nile green moire with exquisite laces and jewels. Miss Beebe wore white*

tulle, the corsage trimmed with silver stars. A few among the many who attended were Miss Clara Winthrop and Miss Margaret Forbes…Supper was served in the dining room at midnight. The walls in this room are of crimson damask, and it was beautifully decorated with flowers, the center piece upon the table being of American beauty roses.

Emily seemed to have many friends. Newspapers reported her presence at multiple weddings, teas and parties for notable Boston girls her age. She traveled extensively and enjoyed nature and new locales. Emily was born into a family that provided her with opportunities and means. And yet, the girl with the silver stars died alone in a hotel room. Luckily, her mother, having died two years prior, did not have to experience the suicide of more than one child. Emily's father, however, was not so lucky. For the last year of his life—he died just over a year after Emily's suicide—J. Arthur was a broken man.

One wonders whether J. Arthur's remaining child, Philip, provided any solace to his father. Born Charles Philip Beebe on January 1, 1884, the Beebe's youngest son was undoubtedly named for J. Arthur's brother, Charles. He chose, like his father, to go by his middle name and often signed letters "C. Philip Beebe." Twelve years younger than Arthur and six years younger than Emily, Philip did not appear in newspaper articles concerning his family. Though his brother and sister were often mentioned, Philip was not. As he was the youngest, he seemed to spend a lot of time on his own.

In an interview with Reverend Smythe's daughter, she told George Moses that Philip was always accompanied by a governess because he was a "problem." Charlotte Nickerson, daughter of Tanglewood's caretaker, had a better impression of Philip. She often found him in the workshop with a "bewildering array of tools." She explained to Moses: "He did seem odd—peculiar, I guess you'd say—to us kids, but we paid no attention to that, and he never objected to our playing about the workshop…In fact, he was always nice and pleasant to us."

Philip entered the Volkmann School in Boston, a prestigious boarding school, to prepare for Harvard. He graduated in 1904. During World War I, the school merged with Nobles and is considered the eighteenth-best preparatory school in the United States. From there, Philip did attend Harvard but only for two years. Apparently he preferred traveling across Europe with his uncle Frank to studying.

Once he returned to America, Philip moved to Mount Hood, Oregon, where he purchased a farm. The 1910 census shows that Philip ran the farm

C. Philip Beebe. Top Row, third from left. *Courtesy of the Noble and Greenough School.*

with two hired hands. He listed his occupation as farmer. His life could not have been more removed from the Boston society life lived by his family, and it seems as if he worked hard to keep distance from his family. When his mother died in 1911, the family questioned whether or not Philip would even show up for the funeral. J. Arthur Beebe wrote to Reverend Smythe, "Philip will be on hand I presume." That comment speaks volumes about the relationship between father and son. Apparently the two did not speak much, not even after a death in the immediate family.

Philip didn't seem to have a close relationship with his sister Emily either. She died in the middle of the summer of 1913, and Reverend Smythe officiated at her service. In October, Philip wrote to the rector and asked casually, "What have you been doing all summer?" The question implies that Philip has not seen Smythe since before the summer and that perhaps he did not attend his sister's funeral. He does not mention his sister's death at all in the letter, but maybe he is trying to remain upbeat. He speaks instead of his own trip out west and of his cousins, George and Esther. He also asks about Falmouth and mentions his plans to return. While his father had given up on Tanglewood, Philip still seemed very interested in their Cape property and even asked about the upkeep of the tennis court.

According to passport and draft registration cards, Philip was nearly six feet tall with blue eyes, brown hair and small features. Curiously, he cites his uncle William Appleton as a source of contact on all of his records and documents instead of his father. In fact, he seemed to have a closer relationship with his extended family than he did with his immediate family. He returned to Boston full time only after his father's death, as if he did not want to live in the same city.

Interestingly enough, J. Arthur Beebe left very little of his substantial fortune to his son, for he believed that his wife's will provided Philip with more than enough money. In fact, he didn't leave Philip any money at all. He wrote in his will, "To my son, Charles Philip Beebe, my large pearl stick pin and blue turquoise mantel clock. I make no further provision for my son, as I believe he has property and income of his own amply sufficient for his needs." Philip did not agree, and he contested his father's will.

While it is true that Mrs. Emily Beebe left Philip a substantial fortune and that he was indeed provided for by his mother's will, it is strange that J. Arthur excluded Philip and gave the majority of his estate (including Tanglewood) to Harvard. Apparently Philip felt the same way, and he was eventually, according to historian Fred Wallace, "awarded $700,000 from his father's estate."

The following year, in 1915, Philip also sought money through his maternal grandfather's trust. The *Boston Daily Globe* reported:

> *On a petition for instruction brought by Francis C. Welch and J. Morris Meredith, trustees under the will of William Appleton, it has been agreed by all parties in interest and confirmed by Judge DeCourcy of the supreme Judicial Court, that a fund of $1, 845.222 held by the trustees shall be distributed equally between William Appleton, a son, and C. Philip Beebe, a grandson of the testator.*

His immense fortune, however, could not solve his personal problems. Like his siblings, he battled some sort of mental collapse. The Boston papers documented various lawsuits involving Philip Beebe. In February 1918, he sued L. Tucker Burr for $50,000, saying that the man made slanderous statements about him in Boston so that "he had been shunned and avoided by men who would otherwise have sought his association." Apparently, before the suit, the Beebe and Burr families had been "very friendly." Another man, Charles Gibson, sued Philip for slander, alleging that Beebe "publicly and falsely accused him of a serious charge which might render him liable to indictment." The case was eventually thrown out. Philip's uncles, Frank Beebe and William Appleton, were considering the actions of their nephew carefully and moved to have him committed to an asylum. Philip fought back and petitioned the courts for his release. The Boston papers reported:

> *Charles Philip Beebe asks to be released from the McLean hospital at Waverley. His petition for a writ of habeas corpus came before Judge Carroll in the Supreme Court yesterday…Mr. Beebe was committed to the hospital as an insane person by the Probate Court a week ago…Mr. Beebe declares he is not insane and is able to take care of his business affairs, that he is not dangerous to himself or others, and that he should no longer be confined at the hospital.*

Another article from the *Evening Globe* reads, "Mr. Beebe [was] willing to testify that while he might be eccentric, he was not insane and he had witnesses willing to testify…The courtroom was crowded and nine analysts were prepared to go on the witness stand and testify as to the mental condition of Beebe." Curiously enough, J. Arthur had been described as "eccentric" as well.

Three weeks later, however, Philip agreed to his uncles' wishes and dropped his efforts for release. The evening edition of the *Boston Globe* reported on December 12, 1919:

> *Action will now be taken by the Suffolk county Probate Court on a petition, filed by the Uncle of Mr. Beebe, that a guardian be appointed to take charge of his business affairs. It is understood that an arrangement has been made so that at intervals, Beebe, with an attendant, may leave the hospital and go to his office on Beacon Street and keep informed as to his fortune, said to amount to about $3,000,000.*

Philip spent a little over the next decade in McLean Hospital, an affiliate of Mass General Hospital, to which he had ironically donated $1,000 only a few years earlier. Interestingly enough, Frank Beebe, who was instrumental in sending his nephew to McLean, died in 1932, and Philip left McLean hospital the same year. By 1933, he purchased the Eastleigh Farm in Framingham, Massachusetts, and returned to the life he began to lead so many years before. According to historian and author Fred Wallace, Philip spent the remainder of his life at Eastleigh and was always accompanied by male attendants from McLean Hospital. He oversaw the operations of the farm and won many awards for his purebred Guernseys. According to Wallace, rumors circulated that Philip's attendants were armed, that he had a mistress and that he killed his secret wife, among other things. Wallace concludes:

> *It appears to this researcher that he was nothing more than a mentally disturbed person. His incarceration in a mental institution was initiated by family members rather than the result of some criminal act. His reclusive behavior probably made him fair game for rumor and innuendo. Unless some other facts come to light, it appears he was just an unfortunate victim of bad genes!*

Perhaps Wallace is right. J. Arthur was also described as eccentric, and his wife was described as depressed. Two of their children committed suicide, and the other was committed to an insane asylum. The vast Appleton and Beebe fortunes could not protect the children from themselves.

J. Arthur spent most of the last year of his life between Frank's home on 30 Beacon Street and the Copley Plaza in Boston—I suppose he simply attempted to go on. The end, for Mr. Beebe, was a quick one. Early in the evening on November 28, 1914, he wandered about the hotel and spoke with various guests. Later, while eating his dinner, he fell forward on the table and died instantly of heart failure. J. Arthur Beebe's life was one of immense fortune and unspeakable tragedy. Fellow Harvard classmate William S. Hall summed up J. Arthur's character and outlook in the following memorial: "Very few in private life had a wider circle of acquaintance. Not many realized that his manner, blithe and debonair, was a veil over tragedies in life that few are called upon to bear. Under the staggering blows which Fate dealt him he kept his feet, and carried himself with manly courage to the end, but with a breaking heart."

J. Arthur Beebe, for all of his suffering, lived almost seventy years. He was survived by his brothers Pierson and Frank, both of whom enjoyed long lives. Their oldest brother, Charles, however, never had the same chance.

Chapter 5

The Forgotten Beebe

Charles Edwin Beebe, the oldest son of James Madison and Esther Elizabeth Beebe, is rarely mentioned in records of any kind. In fact, he died ten years before his brothers began the construction of Highfield and six years before his parents purchased land in Falmouth.

As the oldest child, Charles became a sort of parent to his younger siblings. Charlie, as his brothers and sisters called him, provided entertainment and care for the Beebe children. He helped his sister Mary plant gardens, set off fireworks and balloons to entertain the family on Independence Day, took the family rowing or sailing in his boat, acted as various characters to make his sisters laugh and teased the girls about their attitudes. He and Arthur especially enjoyed when his sisters would bring home their pretty friends. Though Charles did get angry when his sisters disliked the new red stripe on his sailboat or when one of them forgot to bring home dessert, Charles was a caring, paternal and entertaining influence on his siblings. He didn't seem to take himself too seriously and enjoyed having fun.

Charles was an intelligent and talented young man who was recognized for his work. Fannie recalls that on Charles's last day of schooling, "He did not miss in his examination and his original essay on the fine arts which he spoke was commended in the papers." He enjoyed Shakespeare and played the melodeon. Charles planned to open his own store (and follow in his father's business) and toyed with the idea of attending college.

Though he died in France when he was only twenty-seven years old, we can learn a lot about the Beebe family through his words. In the winter and spring of 1859, when Charles was in his twentieth year, he traveled to Paris and kept a brief journal of his trip. In addition to descriptions of his family,

Charles records his voyage aboard the steamer *Europa* and his impressions of France in the mid-nineteenth century.

James Madison Beebe wanted to secure the future of his eldest son and undoubtedly introduced him to influential members of the banking world, the field his son had decided to pursue. Charles's trip to Europe in 1859, while certainly meant to be for pleasure, also seemed to be in part for business. The night before Charles's departure, he and his father stayed up for hours to talk over "business matters," and Charles seemed to relish his father's wisdom. Once abroad, Charles made note of his visits to various offices belonging to friends of Mr. Beebe. During most of the trip, however, he led the elegant life of the elite.

Charles's father was not born into money. In fact, he was working as a dry goods store boy at the age of sixteen, and could only dream of the type of trip abroad on which Charles was about to embark. He worked his way up quickly to acquire the type of wealth that permitted his son the opportunity for many extended European vacations. Charles seems to be well aware of and grateful for his father's sacrifices and expertise. Far from being the stereotypical wealthy parents—aloof and unaffectionate—James and Esther were doting and loving to their children. Charles writes that his mother "did not come down to the depot [to see him off] she felt so bad at my coming away." As Charles stood on the deck of the *Europa* and waved goodbye to his family, he recalled, "Father and Mary [his sister] waved their handkerchiefs. Father seemed to feel badly at my coming away."

Charles and his siblings also seemed to get along well at the time. Before he boarded the steamer, he spent most of his time in New York with his sisters, Mary and Emily. They enjoyed an afternoon walking along the streets and shopping. He describes the "excellent" chocolates they acquired and details their visit to a glass and crockery manufactory. Later on the evening before Charles's departure, they attended a fancy New York party; however, they found the event overcrowded and went back to the hotel to spend time with their parents and younger brother, Frank, instead.

Frank was the youngest Beebe—fourteen years younger than Charles. His older siblings seemed to get a kick out of his sayings and actions, as sister Fannie commented in her journals. Charles writes that his six-year-old brother was in no way moved by the impending trip abroad. "Frankie did not mind it much. He was eating an orange in the parlor and could scarcely find the time to say goodbye." One can just imagine the Lord of Highfield, Frank Beebe himself, as little Frankie eating his orange without a care in the world.

New York, 1860. *Jacobsteinafm.*

Frank Beebe playing chess.
Courtesy of Department of Special Collections and University Archives. Stanford University Libraries.

The *Europa* set sail for Liverpool on February 2, 1859. Once in Liverpool, Charles planned to ride into London and stay with family friends for a day before the trip to Paris. The voyage overseas lasted thirteen days, seven of which were extremely rough. Charles describes, "An old western squall kept us rolling terribly all night and there was one lurch which made havoc with all the crockery. Nearly all on board were sick." He goes on to say, "The roll last night was very severe. Mr. Morgan…was walking for exercise when a sudden lurch threw him off his feet and carried him under a settee, scraping his leg so badly that he was put under the care of a surgeon." With the terrible weather came fog, which made the voyage quite dangerous. At one point toward the end of the trip, the ship narrowly escaped a collision with land by about ten minutes.

Due to the extreme weather conditions, the ladies remained below deck and were often ill throughout the trip. Charles mentioned them often and lamented that he was "pent up" in the saloon all day with the gentlemen. They read, smoked, played the fiddle, told stories and sang, but Charles joked that the entertainment lacked "talents or voices." Others played popular card games such as euchre and whist. Charles preferred to be out on the deck taking in as much activity as possible and remarked that "exercise at sea keeps the body in good condition."

Once the *Europa* reached Liverpool, Charles rode to London with friends. After a brief stay, he was slated to meet up with his sister Fannie and his brother Pierson (whose name Charles writes as "Pearson") who were already in France at the time. Though the Beebe children often traveled abroad with their parents, as they got older they traveled with one another. Charles was later than expected, after his stop off in London, and his siblings stayed up late that evening to make sure their brother arrived safely. He writes, "Fannie rushed to the door and seemed very glad to see me."

Charles, Fannie and Pierson (who Charles sometimes called Eddie) were all close in age and enjoyed each other's company immensely during this particular trip. Charles and Pierson walked through the city of Paris, and Fannie joined them for various church services, parties and balls.

After reading Charles's diary entries, one realizes his love for music and, above all, dancing. In fact, he was quite disappointed with one evening because "there was no room to dance or do anything and no one to play either." He found the night "rather stupid." On another occasion, he was surprised that he had a good time because he didn't get much of an opportunity to dance. Yet, he attended many fine parties throughout his trip, the highlight of which was the Grand Ball for the Americans, for which his sister Fannie had purchased a "new tarleton" to wear. He writes, "The

The American Ball, Hotel Du Louvre, 1856. Illustrated London News.

Strauss Band composed of forty pieces played, and very finely. Refreshments were passed around continually. The room looked charmingly. So many gas lights and gay bodies. It was a beautiful sight. Came home at 3 AM."

Charles enjoyed dancing with the ladies at the various events he attended while in Paris, and he kept a record of his partners. There was Sally Hayward, whom he found "very bright"; Miss Maer, with whom he danced "considerable"; Miss Cummings; Miss Whitewell; Miss Wilson; Miss Raffe; and Mrs. Clifton. He even enjoyed dancing with his sister Fannie and the "little ones." He was amused that Miss Hayward had never heard of round dances—dances led by a person who calls out the steps in advance. And he joked that he danced his best polka for the better part of a half of an hour while trying to dress aboard the lurching steamer.

As noted, Charles was particularly fond of the ladies during this trip. While on the ship, he was dismayed that they spent so much time below deck due to the tumultuous conditions at sea. He wrote that Miss Goodwin was "very agreeable" and Miss Sturges was "very bright." As the trip progressed, however, Miss Goodwin seems to have won out. Charles mentioned her repeatedly. He worried over her seasickness and "thin" condition. When she recovered, they played forty games of backgammon together. Even though she won, Charles wrote that he "never felt better." They also partnered up for a raffle aboard ship.

Once the ship docked, and he parted company with Miss Goodwin, Charles focused his attention on a new young lady whom he referred to as

"Miss Maer." When in Paris, she accompanied him to the Grand Ball for the Americans at the Louvre, where they had a "splendid time." She also joined him at other events, such as the marionettes.

While Frank and Pierson Beebe shared their brother's love for ladies, dancing and music—they attended many elite Boston parties together—neither of them ever married. Only brother J. Arthur took that final step. One wonders, had he been given the chance, what path Charles would have taken.

The city of Paris provided much joy for Charles, Fannie and Pierson. Though he hesitated to "judge in so short a time," Charles found London "dark and dirty" (much as Pip in Dickens's classic novel *Great Expectations*). In contrast, he relished the "lively and cheerful" sights and people of Paris, commenting that it was "the gayest place [he] ever saw." His tastes were not confined to the city, however, and he, like his siblings, was devoted to the beauties of nature as well.

After his arrival in Liverpool, Charles took the road to London, which he called "delightful all the way" for it "abounded in beautiful scenery." Once in London, he made it a point to visit Hyde Park, but it was February and "gloomy." The season thwarted his plans in Paris as well. The trees had yet to bloom in the Garden of the Tuileries. Yet, to his delight, the Bois de Bologne was "one of the grand sights of Paris." Had he lived, he surely would have sought solace from the city on acreage similar to Beebe Woods. And, like his brothers, he most certainly would have built a grand residence for himself—one to rival Highfield and Tanglewood. He marveled at his friends

Bois de Boulogne. *Casas-Rodriguez Collection.*

the Morgans' "magnificent" estate in London and remarked that it was in "the best style and all as neat as wax." The highlight of Charles's trip to Paris involved the apartments at the Luxembourg: "[I] saw the most beautiful apartments I ever laid eyes on. Magnificent frescoes. I saw the Emperor's reception room, the Senate Chamber, the sleeping apartment of Catherine de Medici, and the chapel where the Emperor worships. All elegant."

For all their revelries and extravagances, however, the Beebes' greatest love was a simple one. God came foremost in their lives. Charles attended regular church services throughout this trip. Aboard the *Europa*, the captain officiated when the weather cooperated. Charles wrote, "Captain Leitch read the Episcopal Service this forenoon, and all the sailors marched in dressed in their best suits. It really was an impressive and interesting sight, and some seemed to be impressed with the solemnity of the occasion. They all had their books before them and the service was quite long."

While in Paris, he often attended the American chapel, which he found "neat but too large." He did not find the sermons very appealing either. He was far more impressed with his experience at the Hotel des Invalides:

Hotel des Invalides, Paris.
Edouard Baldus.

The Madeleine, Paris. *Edouard Baldus.*

> *Enjoyed the service very much. The organ was very sweet and played well. A fine band is also stationed in the gallery and they favored us with a waltz as one piece. A lot of old infirm soldiers marched in and lined the passage to the altar, about ten boy drummers ahead of them, who did their part well. The service being through, the soldiers were reviewed in the courtyard. It was an impressive scene all through.*

Interested in the architecture of the Catholic churches, Charles attended a couple masses during his stay. While he was most certainly impressed with the structures, especially the Madeleine, he was critical of the services and confided in his diary, "I am not pleased with the Catholic service, but consider it a mass of mummery and really pity the people. But they seem to be more devoted to their religion than other people I know."

No doubt he would have helped his brothers and sisters in their campaign to build St. Barnabus—the historic and beautiful Episcopal church on the green in Falmouth. Though he died in France a mere seven years after his journals were written, Charles is memorialized in Falmouth, like so many of the Beebes, as a permanent reminder of their influence and devotion, not only to their God, but to their sanctuary here on earth.

Chapter 6

RANDLE'S REMEDIES

In every one of my lectures I shall praise Falmouth. You will never be able to accommodate the summer people who will be attracted here by my fine publicity.
—Helen Gertrude Randle

Sixty-six years after Charles's death, the last of the Beebe children died. Frank Beebe's passing in 1932 officially ended his family's reign on the hill.

Another man of fortune was about to become involved with the Beebe estates, and he shared a lot in common with Frank Beebe. Edgar H. Bristol had been summering on Cape Cod with his family for almost twenty years by the time of Frank Beebe's death. Like Pierson and J. Arthur Beebe, E.H. Bristol and his brother built large homes in Falmouth. They preferred the ocean to the woods and occupied portions of the Heights beach area.

E.H., as everyone called him, had owned the Foxboro Company with his brother since 1908. Moses writes of Bristol's company and ingenuity:

> *The Foxboro Company, originally a manufacturer of all sorts of pressure and temperature gauges, became a notable leader in perfecting automatic controls by industrial instruments. And E.H., the company's president from the outset, was greatly responsible for that leadership, authoring some 40 patents, some so basic in character as to establish entirely new principles of instrument design and operation. To say that he was a genius in his field would be no exaggeration.*

E.H. was more than a genius, however; he was an optimist with an unfailing faith in humanity. In 1922, he founded the New Civilization movement. The movement, which had over one thousand members, was based on the idea that people are inherently good and will act as their conscience dictates. To test his theory, Bristol ran buses equipped with coin boxes. Those who rode the buses only had to pay if they felt the ride was worthy, and even then, they didn't have to pay unless they wanted to do so. He planned to open a public hospital and community center, and guests would only pay what their consciences dictated. On the same idea, he would install a pay phone with no slot. E.H. was no fool, and he believed that his idea was pragmatic. He told newspapers of the day, "I am interested in only that which is economically sound."

Today, winter and summer residents alike know Bristol Beach, an extension of the Heights located at the end of Maravista Avenue. Much like the beach he donated to Falmouth or the New Civilization movement he founded, E.H. Bristol longed to provide solace to his fellow man. He sought a place where residents could go for relaxation and health. He realized his dream when he opened the Falmouth Institute—a spa of sorts—where citizens could go to refresh and renew their physical and mental well being. The institute was to be housed at Highfield through a contract with the Beebe heirs. While the first couple of years were not very successful, and Bristol altered the intent of the institute—adding research labs at Tanglewood and running a sort of retirement hotel at Highfield—the summer of 1936 gave Bristol a cause for new hope in the form of Helen Randle.

Little did Bristol know that the woman in whom he placed so much hope was a total fraud and perhaps even mentally disturbed. At the very least, she was self-motivated and deceitful. In fact, while Edgar H. Bristol was making his fortune, Randle was formulating get-rich schemes and swindling hundreds of people all along the East Coast. She was a very busy lady, indeed, even before her escapades in Falmouth. It is really too bad that such a genuine man as Bristol crossed paths with such a disingenuous woman as Helen Randle.

During her criminal career, Randle touted herself as an expert on a variety of topics: astrology, nutrition and charm, to name a few. She impersonated naval officials, scammed brokerage firms, touted false degrees and posed as a licensed physician. She took part in mail fraud, attempted kidnapping and bogus lawsuits. After years of running from authorities and preying on the citizens in every town along the way, Randle never seemed cognizant of the destruction she left behind, or perhaps she never cared. More often than not, she was arrested for practicing medicine without a license.

While she appeared in November 1934 to give the opening address at the convention of the Florida Astrological Association as "one of the outstanding figures in the astrological field," Randle realized quickly that she would make little money from the constellations. She had already begun, in the early 1930s, to promote herself from Florida to New York as a lecturer of health topics, a food dietician, a masterful mind and body builder, a psychologist and a personality analyst. And there was certainly money to be made in these areas. In fact, with recent headlines like "Flordia Health Spas Emphasize that You are What You Eat," Randle could still promote her "Sun and Diet Spa" on the internet today and make a fortune.

Helen Gertrude Randle. *Courtesy of the* Falmouth Enterprise.

Just prior to her arrival in Massachusetts, Randle fled her mountain cottage in Gettysburg, Pennsylvania, where she administered her "treatments." In the process of evading yet another arrest, she left a crippled Lancaster girl in the cottage. The American Red Cross was alerted by police who took custody of the girl. Randle had set up shop in Gettysburg after her arrest in Montgomery, Alabama. Police chased her across nine states over warrants issued at Ocean City, New Jersey, where she was wanted for practicing medicine without a license.

Still, over the years, Randle surely acquired some knowledge of proper diet and nutrition. In fact, she co-authored two books on the subject in 1934 through her own publication company, Helen Randle Health Publications out of Greenville, South Carolina: *The Proper Diet for Every Case of Impaired Health, With General Suggestions Regarding Health and Combination of Foods, Together with Valuable Food Formula* and *Feeding the Family Health Cook Book.* These books are still housed in major libraries and even listed on Amazon.

Randle advocated a diet in which the proper foods and the proper combination of foods would lead to overall health. In an interview she gave in October 1934, she told the *Abilene Morning News* in Texas that "America is the sickest nation in the world because Americans are overfed and undernourished…Moderation in eating as well as in other things in life would be looked upon as a sign of culture and good breeding…Everyone could be healthy and keep well if they would only fast intelligently." While her advice sounds innocent enough, in the same article, she went on to claim that she served as the private dietician for President Woodrow Wilson, Mahatma Gandhi, Queen Marie of Rumania, Queen Dwight Morrow, Kaiser Wilhelm, Maria of Yugoslavia and many Hollywood stars. She actually said of William Jennings Bryan, secretary of state under Woodrow Wilson, "It was impossible to keep him from eating huge steaks and drinking quarts of coffee before retiring." She also claimed to have come up with a diet for Gandhi that consisted of a twenty-one-day fast. Whether Randle believed her own lies, suffered from mental illness or knowingly duped others, the lies were certainly outlandish, and they certainly came easily.

Her knowledge of diet, combined with Randle's many other charms, ensured some success. According to Moses, Harry B. Ivers of Wareham attended one of Helen Randle's lectures while he was in Florida and was impressed enough to seek treatment. Doctors had told Ivers that he had a matter of weeks to live, so Randle's promise to cure every ailment provided him with much needed hope. Since Ivers lived for another decade, his meeting with Helen Randle probably had very little to do with his recovery. One wonders about the "doctors" he had consulted in Florida. While Randle simply prescribed a diet for Ivers, he was convinced that Randle's diet secrets were responsible for his recovery and well being. With all the best intentions, he brought her to Massachusetts. As head of the Southeastern Massachusetts Chamber of Commerce, he used his influence to introduce Randle to a new audience of victims, and in the summer of 1936, she began a series of lectures in Southeastern Massachusetts.

With her smoky eyes and seductive curves, the young woman wowed audiences through her stories of dietary prescriptions. A persuasive speaker, Randle charmed men and women alike. While females were interested in her tricks for slimming down and attracting husbands, men were duped by her well-staged sex appeal. George Moses was a young reporter for the *Falmouth Enterprise* when he covered Randle's lectures. He supplies an amusing anecdote on one of her performances: "She let a sequin wrap slip from her shoulders to reveal a low-cut black velvet gown (and what was encased in it) [and] the all-male, mostly middle-aged audience sat up and took even closer notice."

Randle was certainly an intelligent, cultured and attractive woman. Had she stuck to dietary lectures, she might have made a decent name for herself and earned an adequate and honest living. In fact, one of the only facts we know about Randle is that at one point she taught public speaking and methods of English at Clemson College in South Carolina. Surely, she was a talented and persuasive speaker. If only she had chosen the honest route. Randle, however, was not passionate about the advice she peddled; she was passionate about money, lots of money. Once she arrived in Massachusetts, she did not take long to set her sights on Highfield and Tanglewood.

Randle pitched her Sun and Diet School model to Bristol, who eagerly sought a permit to employ her system at Highfield—a system that, as stated previously, pretty much guaranteed the cure for every aliment or disease that plagued the human body. Randle's promise to cure all should have been a clue to Bristol that all was not well, but Mrs. Randle was certainly persuasive, and Bristol bought into her promises.

The Beebe mansions lacked modern luxuries (Highfield had no heat), and both needed extensive repairs. Because Bristol and Randle wanted to bring in guests from New Bedford right away, they housed them at Highfield while they began work on Tanglewood. They planned to restore Highfield after completing Tanglewood.

Meanwhile, Randle publicized her program in Falmouth through advertisements and lectures. She spoke with local business owners whom she talked into promoting and carrying her fruits and vegetables. She met with the heirs of the Beebe estate and bought interest in Tanglewood and Highfield (or at least that is what she told the *Falmouth Enterprise*). In an article dated November 12, 1936, she promoted and explained her Sun and Diet system to Falmouth residents, "This is not a hospital or a sanatorium, but a school for instruction in right living. 'Eat your way to health' is the theme which combines correct diet with a right-thinking attitude toward life, together with a program of amusement and education." In the same article, she promised to fly back and forth between her properties in Florida and the Carolinas in her private plane (which hadn't been built yet, of course). She described the mineral gardens that would replace the Beebe gardens and transform the fruits and vegetables planted in their soil.

Yet while Helen Randle was busy touting her Sun and Diet program, her past was slowly catching up with her. Patrolman John Nolan stopped a car driven by Randle's eighteen-year-old secretary Helen J. Beckett in Fairhaven, Massachusetts. Randle and her secretary were on their way to Falmouth where Helen was slated to speak. Officer Nolan charged Beckett with speeding and driving without a license and brought her to the New Bedford district court. Days later, he arrested Randle herself, who was wanted on charges of illegally practicing medicine in Wareham. Randle promised the state trooper that she would appear in court that Thursday. She must have been very charming, as he obliged her. Of course, when she never showed up, Nolan was subject to the same sick feeling this "healer" left with everyone who trusted her. The November 30 edition of the *Fitchburg Sentinel* read, "Health Camp Operator Fails to Appear for Trial." Bristol, however, still believed in Randle and posted her bail to the tune of $1,000.

In the weeks that followed, Bristol also accompanied Randle on visits to the Carolinas and Florida, where he supplied capital for her ventures. Meanwhile in Falmouth, suspicions mounted. The editor of the *Enterprise*, George Hough, investigated Randle's activities, and it didn't take him long to discover her dishonest dealings. The chief of police in Wareham received an anonymous tip to check up on Randle's activities in Gettysburg. Dr. Oscar S. Simpson of Falmouth wrote the following note to the chief of police in Gettysburg, Pennsylvania: "Have you any information which you can give me concerning one Mrs. Helen G. Randle, who has come to this town supposedly to operate a sun and diet health camp. She is involved in a legal action concerning the illegal practice of medicine."

Of course, they had plenty of information on Mrs. Randle, who fled Gettysburg after lecturing and practicing medicine illegally there as well. With evidence from multiple states, the *Falmouth Enterprise* exposed Helen Randle in its December 10 article titled "Diet Leader's Many Claims Bring Scrutiny of Her Proofs and Past." The article opened:

> *No less striking than the extravagance of Helen Gertrude Randle's claims is the scarcity of facts to back them up. If Mrs. Randle is "America's leading dietetic expert," the story of her rise to that pinnacle ought to be easily accessible in many standard sources of information. On the contrary it has taken exhaustive research on the part of The Falmouth Enterprise to gather the story that is reported here. Odd, indeed, are some of the testimonials with which Mrs. Randle buttresses her assertion of unique health-giving secrets; strange are some of the associations revealed.*

The article goes on to say that a friend of E.H. Bristol had gone to great lengths to investigate the woman in whom his friend was placing so much trust and money. In the beginning of the article, the *Enterprise* reviews the trouble in Wareham and the charges against Mrs. Randle. Next, the reporter reviews her introduction to Falmouth and her many outrageous claims. The article continues:

> *According to Mrs. Randle, she is "one of America's if not one of the world's leaders in research work in dietetics and food chemistry," "America's most masterful mind and body builder," "internationally known author, lecturer, teacher." But According to the Bureau of Investigation of the American Medical Association, "A careful search of all available records—and ours are pretty complete—failed to show that Helen Gertrude Randle is in any sense an authority on the subjects she claims to know."*

The *Enterprise* also exposed her false medical and college degrees as well as her bogus endorsements from supposed doctors. After a thorough write up of her disingenuous claims, the paper examined her Sun and Diet programs:

> *Let us look at her Sun and Diet health resorts. The first one was opened in Asherville [*sic*], North Carolina, about June, 1935, and closed in August, 1936. The second opened early this year in Hendersonville and was closed in October. In October came announcement of a new winter resort in Avon Park, Florida. According to Mrs. Randle her Sun and Diet resorts occupy "a most unusual position in being able to not only correct the cause of so-called impaired health, but to prevent the ravages of so-called disease on the human body." In her resort treatments Mrs. Randle uses (and has said she would use at Falmouth)—1, Sunshine in the form of sun baths; 2, Mineralized fruits and vegetables…; 3, Massage therapy; 4, Relaxation and corrective physical culture; 5, Right thinking and a harmonious attitude toward life, together with a well-formed program for interest, amusement and education of the individual.*

The *Enterprise* further reported that Mrs. Randle failed to pay her rent or her employees at these resorts and fled when her landlady and workers went to the police. In fact, Mrs. Randle often fled before authorities could arrest her; that being said, she was arrested many times before she came to Falmouth. However, in an interview with the *Enterprise* after her arrest in Wareham, Randle stated, "I have never been arrested before. In the South it's a disgrace to be arrested." The explosive article concluded with the following:

> *But the test of Mrs. Randle is something more than the rich melodious southern voice with which she greets her audience and the charm of her*

personality which she is not loathe to suggest come from her mastery of diets and Helen Randle's "beauty and charm cocktails." The test is the record of what lies behind her pretensions. That is the record which is reported here.

Apparently that record was not enough to sway E.H. Bristol. He remained devoted to Mrs. Randle and their shared vision until his friends did further research into her character. Once they confronted Bristol with evidence of Randle's various husbands and other sordid affairs, Bristol finally conceded that Randle had been dishonest, and he decided to withdraw his financial support.

COOKS UP SUIT

With the filing of attachments totalling $600,000 at Dedham, Mass., Mrs. Helen G. Randle (right), nutrition expert, indicated she planned to sue Edgar H. Bristol, wealthy manufacturer, for damages in that amount, alleging breach of contract in connection with the operation of diet resorts at Falmouth, Mass., and Avon Park, Fla. She claims she and Bristol went through a marriage ceremony at New York in 1936.

Helen Randle's suit. *The* Evening Gazette, *1937.*

In January 1937, Randle returned to Massachusetts. According to Randle, Bristol was supposed to meet her at the train station in Boston. Instead, he sent his lawyer who brought Randle to the authorities. Bristol released the $1,000 bond he had posted for Randle's earlier bail. Shocked but undeterred, Randle posted her own bail and planned her revenge.

Soon papers across the country reported Randle's intentions to sue Bristol for $600,000 for breach of contract, deception and seduction. She claimed that she owned half stock in the properties at Avon Park and Falmouth and that Bristol promised her a yearly income of $50,000. Randle went further and even dared to assert that she was Bristol's wife. She claimed that the two were married by a notary public at the Waldorf Astoria in New York. Of course Bristol, who was already married, denied these claims. Randle was basically forced out of Falmouth by the citizens of the town and decided to give up the suit altogether. She'd take her chances elsewhere.

Curiously, Randle may have been responsible for one fine addition to Highfield Hall. In his report on Highfield, Maximilian Ferro noted:

> *At the first landing, we find three little but incredibly lovely windows of relatively modern floral pattern stained glass. Among all of the house's laudable features, these are my sentimental favorite, and it is tempting though probably incorrect to ascribe this little embellishment to Helen Gertrude Randall, the glamorous crook who was the mansion's most colorful past occupant.*

After her bout in Falmouth, Helen Randle moved on to other scams. She changed her name to Rosalyn Randle and touted her regime in other cities. Knowing how lucrative "health care" was at the time, she did not give up on her medical practice. In fact, she promoted it at all costs. Take the case of Rufus Reed.

Highfield interior. *Photo by author.*

In December 1938, months after she left Falmouth, Randle was arrested in Washington, D.C., for obtaining $500 from Mrs. Catherine H. Reed—a fee for curing Reed's son, Rufus. Rufus was a university student at the University of Pennsylvania. Randle told the mother that her son had a suicide complex and a "malformation of the brain." Randle assured Mrs. Rufus that she could treat the boy's weak will and unbalanced mind. According to the *Frederick Post* in Maryland, Randle told Rufus that "she could improve his mental health, put him ahead in his studies and even make him grow taller." The article continued:

> [Randle] *is said to have told the mother she had handled similar cases before, and had effected a cure in the case of the heir to a large fortune and had been retained by the wealthy family to accompany him to the Island of Crete. Mrs. Randle also allegedly told the mother that university authorities had sent her a picture of Rufus' brain in which, she said, a malformation was shown and that, if he were placed in her care, she could and would prescribe a certain diet which would slow down the brain of the boy and give him a chance to develop properly. In furtherance of the alleged false pretenses, according to the grand jury, Miss Randle said she would give the boy a certain mental treatment to correct the mental ills from which he was suffering and that for $500 she would cure the boy and bring him back to normal conditions.*

Randle pleaded not guilty to the charge, claiming that it stemmed from a desire to humiliate her. The plea sounds familiar, as she used versions of it many times in the past. In a previous case, Randle submitted that a man threatened to give her "ugly publicity." When arraigned in Middleboro, Massachusetts, in November 1936, she claimed that "jealousy on the part of the medical profession" was responsible for her arrest.

By 1939, Randle changed her business plan slightly and started selling her expertise in an additional area on which she truly was an expert: charm. While she never took courses in charm or held any degrees, she successfully managed to fool most of the eastern seaboard for almost a decade through her charm.

In addition to altering her business plan by 1939, Randle also took a break from the lecture circuit and used the post to advertise. In April 1939, the *Gettysburg Times* reported on Randle's new activities:

> *Recently, Mrs. Randle was indicted again, on eight counts of using the mail to defraud. She was charged with mailing claims that she was a*

INCREASE YOUR INCOME

Develop Your Personality

Learn to Live Effectively

Rosalyn Randle, A. B., M. N.

Rosalyn Randle has trained more men and women to talk and live effectively than any other living woman

★ ★ ★

FREE

Demonstration Lecture

by

ROSALYN RANDLE

A. B., M. N.

"Put your Best Self Forward"

Francis Scott Key Hotel

Ball Room

Wednesday, Thursday, Friday

Feb. 9, 10, 11, at 8 P. M.

15 Things this training will help you do . . .

The Rosalyn Randle Course in Effective Speaking and Personality Development will help you to:

1. THINK ON YOUR FEET and speak extemporaneously before business conferences, clubs, organizations, dinners.

2. DEVELOP COURAGE AND SELF-CONFIDENCE. Destroy fear. Cure an inferiority complex.

3. INCREASE YOUR POISE, polish and personal force both in business interviews and before groups.

4. "SELL" YOURSELF, YOUR SERVICES, your product, your enthusiasm.

5. WIN MORE FRIENDS by increasing your knowledge of practical psychology, your skill in human relations.

6. IMPROVE YOUR MEMORY, speak without notes and recall names and faces.

7. WRITE MORE EFFECTIVE LETTERS.

8. ENRICH YOUR COMMAND OF ENGLISH.

9. READ MORE WORTHWHILE BOOKS.

10. BECOME A LEADER in your business or pgofession through your ability to speak.

11. BECOME A MORE ENTERTAINING CONVERSATIONALIST.

12. INCREASE YOUR INCOME by developing the ability to handle people. John D. Rockefeller, Sr., once said, "I will pay more for the ability to handle people than for any other ability under the sun."

13. INSPIRE YOU WITH NEW IDEAS. You will participate in and listen to talks that will broaden your interest and jar you out of a rut.

14. KNOW INTIMATELY MANY AMBITIOUS MEN AND WOMEN. In these classes you will form friendships that will last a lifetime.

15. DEVELOP YOUR LATENT POWERS and improve your personality. Professor William James of Harvard declared that the average man developes only 10 per cent. of his mental powers.

ADMIT TWO

(While Seats are Available)

Opening Session of the Rosalyn Randle Course in Effective Speaking and Personality development:

Francis Scott Key Hotel

Ballroom

Wednesday, Feb. 9 at 8 P. M.

This announcement will not appear again. Tear out this coupon now. If you can't use it yourself, why not pass it along to a friend?

Rosalyn Randle Institute of Effective Speaking

Human Relations and Personality Building

2400 16th St., N. W. Washington, D. C. Columbia 8838

Rosalyn Randle advertisement. *Courtesy of the* Frederick News Post.

graduate of many universities, had a long career in many healing sciences, could cure most diseases, had treated 1,000 persons without failure, could teach immunity to all diseases and stipulated that her clients must pay $500 dollars in advance.

Claiming she was ill and under a physician's care, Randle never made it to her trial in a District of Columbia court, where she was charged with obtaining money under false pretenses. She used the excuse that she had been in a car accident to skip out on a different trial. Same track record. She either disappeared or sent excuses. When she finally appeared before the court in late April 1939, she rescinded her guilty pleas and accused a

North Carolina judge of forcing her to admit to practicing medicine illegally. She told Justice Jesse C. Adkins in a Washington, D.C. courtroom, "I was railroaded into pleading guilty to that charge. It was all a plot against me. I wasn't guilty." Assistant United States Attorney Arthur B. Caldwell surprised Randle by calling the judge and many other witnesses to the stand to contradict Randle's testimony. Caldwell nailed Randle in repeated lies or evasive responses. Here is a portion of the text from that trial:

> *"Were you placed on probation for two years, Mrs. Randle?" Caldwell asked.*
> *"I don't remember."*
> *"You mean to say you don't remember whether you were placed on probation?" Justice Jesse C. Adkins asked.*
> *"I'll be glad to refresh her recollection," Caldwell said. "Is Mrs. Warren Mitchell in the court room?"*
> *One of the spectators arose in the rear of the room.*
> *"Do you recognize your probation officer, Mrs. Randle?" Caldwell asked.*
> *The witness shook her head.*
> *To contradict her testimony that she had taught dietetics, psychology and hygiene at Clemson College, in Clemson, South Carolina, Caldwell placed F.H.A. Calhoun, dean of the school, on the stand.*
> *"What did she teach in your school?" Caldwell asked.*
> *"She taught public speaking and methods of English."*
> *"Did she ever teach dietetics, psychology or hygiene?"*
> *"No. We don't have a course in dietetics there."*

Although she testified she had studied dietetics and nutrition at three universities, Mrs. Randle admitted under cross-examination that she had not registered in any of these courses. She maintained she attended the lectures, however.

> *"You honor," Caldwell asked, "I should like to read into the records this excerpt from the regulations of the University of Virginia, one of the schools where Mrs. Randle attended lectures in courses for which she never registered: 'No student will be admitted to any course without a properly signed registration card.'"*

Her blatant lies and numerous trials did not deter her. Not long after the trial quoted above, Randle was arrested again on a charge of false pretense. While serving eight months in Washington, D.C., Randle was tried yet again in the

United States District Court there for numerous charges of fraud. Though Judge James W. Morris only placed her on probation, he gave her what the *Gettysburg Times* called a "tongue lashing" first. Morris warned Randle, "You must stop this practice…It is something that shocks one to think the credulity and pathetic hope of those suffering from incurable disease be played upon for profit. I promise you that a strict surveillance will be maintained over your activities. Any breach of conduct will mean jail for you."

The newspaper noted Randle's response and her bleak future: "With tears in her eyes, Miss Randle promised to reform. But freedom is still a long way off. She has six more months to serve on the first conviction and Texas authorities are waiting to take her to their state to try her on a similar charge there."

At that trial, Randle dropped a bombshell—one that this author assumed was just another of her many lies until I investigated further. She told the judge that she could not go to prison because she was the sole support of a twelve-year-old daughter. She begged the judge for mercy. A daughter? I was floored. Where was this daughter throughout the previous decade of Randle's other trials, her lectures and her scams? She surely was not located at any of the so-called spas, and there was never any mention of her on Cape Cod.

Rosalyn Randle advertisement. *Courtesy of the* Frederick News Post.

In fact, no matter what first name she used, Randle often went by Mrs. Randle, yet no one could find any evidence of a husband, never mind a daughter. According to George Moses, one of the final straws for E.H. Bristol was the fact that Randle lied about a string of husbands. Though Bristol was already married and had no interest in marrying Randle, he probably finally chose to face the same issue I have faced in my research. If Randle was willing to lie about her personal life, why would she be honest elsewhere? Bristol truly believed in and defended Randle, and I think his anger stemmed from her betrayal of that trust. Moses writes,

> *E.H. joined* [Randle] *at their jointly-held resort in Avon Park and was guest of honor at a gala New Year's Eve party. When he returned home his concerned friends were ready and waiting with even more ammunition. She'd admitted to one husband (drowned, she claimed). But they had dug up another one—in Norristown, Pennsylvania, and just maybe another—or was it the same one?—in Jacksonville, Florida.*

In fact, I did find a husband and daughter in Jacksonville, Florida. In 1929, Thomas Randle, Helen and Helen's daughter, Eunice Rosalyn, lived at 703 Laura Street. According to records, Eunice was born in 1928. At the time, Randle managed a local inn, the Laurel Inn. In 1930, she went by the name Gertrude Randle. By 1931, Helen lived in the same spot with her daughter Eunice, but Thomas was no longer there. Through further investigation, I found a divorce record for Thomas and Helen dated 1930. By 1944, a Supreme Court case in North Carolina clearly shows that Eunice's father was deceased and left property to his daughter (which, of course, Helen tried to steal). I cannot find a death record before 1944 for Thomas Randle. Therefore, Helen had a child in 1928—perhaps the father was Randle, perhaps not.

Though there is no mention of Randle's daughter or husband in most of the newspaper articles on the infamous woman, I found two entries, as well as court records, that validate their existence. Randle may have had many husbands, as the residents of Falmouth astutely observed. In the July 8, 1933 issue of the *Star and Sentinel*, the newspaper reports, "Mr. and Mrs. Randle have rented a cottage at Caledonia for the summer." At that point, Randle was divorced from Thomas, so who was with her at the cottage? Did she even really have a husband with her, or was she trying to keep her divorce quiet? Certainly, it wouldn't be the first time she had lied to reporters.

The evidence of Randle's husbands took another strange twist when I found a marriage through genealogy records for Helen Gertrude Randle and Joseph Leclerc in 1926 in Greenwood, South Carolina—a place which Helen Gertrude Randle frequented. Her daughter was born in 1928, at which time she was married to Thomas Randle. In fact, she would have had to have been married to Thomas Randle prior to her marriage to Leclerc in 1926. Apparently, she was married to two men at the same time. At first, I threw the idea out and assumed there were two Helen Gertrude Randles running around Greenwood, and that is still a possibility, but I stumbled upon more concrete evidence.

First of all, multiple genealogy trees on ancestry.com show Eunice Rosalyn Randle's mother (Helen Gertrude) as the wife of Joseph LeClerc. LeClerc is not Eunice's father. Secondly, in these records Randle is listed as Helen Gertrude Davis Randle LeClerc. Davis, by all accounts, is Randle's maiden name. In fact, she co-wrote one of her books with two Davis relatives, and she gave her address as that of Ms. Lilian G. Davis. While I'm willing to concede that there could be two Helen Gertrude Randles, I am far less willing to concede that there were two Helen Gertrude Davis Randles living in the same place at the same time, though anything is possible. To further complicate matters, Randle told newspapers in 1938 that she and E.H. Bristol were married in New York in the late 1930s, but LeClerc didn't die until 1956. I don't believe for a second that E.H. Bristol (who was already married himself) married Randle, but the fact that she would accuse Bristol of marrying her while she may have been already married is very disturbing (though after all I have researched on Ms. Randle, I am not surprised).

Randle did, in fact, have a daughter. Not only do I have the census records, but I actually found a photograph of the two together. In the May 29, 1936 edition of the *Oakland Tribune*, Helen Randle is pictured with her daughter at the chiropractic convention she attended almost annually. Usually, Helen spoke at these conventions, and she was interviewed a number of times prior to these speaking engagements. There is no doubt that the woman in the picture is the same Helen Randle who came to Falmouth that summer. With all of the fraudulent medicine she was practicing and all of the phony lectures she was giving, Helen obviously did not spend much time with her child. No one in Falmouth even knew that Randle had a child.

The next mention I found of Helen Randle and her daughter is what seems to be Helen's attempt to kidnap Eunice. In 1943, an article in the *Herald Journal* titled "Former Greenville Sheriff Faces Impersonation Charge" describes how former sheriff Carlos Rector and Helen Randle "impersonated officials of the office of price administration and purchasing agents of the navy department." The article further explains, "Eunice

Randle, 15, reported them after Rector tried to get her to go into his car on her way to school. Randle was denied custody of her daughter last year." The article goes on to say that Eunice lived in Greenville with Helen's mother.

If I were to be kind, I'd assume Helen loved and wanted her daughter back. However, Eunice's father left his daughter property. As the girl was not eighteen years of age, her guardian was to take charge of said property. Helen obviously wanted custody of her daughter so that she could have access to the poor girl's property. Not only that, but the man who helped her attempt to kidnap her own daughter had just gotten out of jail himself. For what? For murdering the former sheriff. The more I researched, the more disturbed I was by Randle's character.

The woman was certainly motivated by money, but I think there was more. She did it for the thrill—to be in front of the crowd and fool the masses. She was brazen in her attempts. The last I read of Randle in the newspapers is in July 1943 when Helen gave a lecture sponsored by the Gettysburg Mothers' club. She touted herself as a noted dietician, psychologist and food expert in the very place where she was exposed, the very place she fled only three years earlier. This time, she didn't even bother to change her name.

Hear! Rosalyn Randle

A. B., B. S.

Tell you how . . . to have a charming PERSONALITY . . KEEP YOUTH AND ENERGY . . . MAKE FRIENDS . . . HAVE PERFECT HEALTH . . . BE SUCCESSFUL . . . STREAMLINE YOUR FIGURE . . . DRESS WITH CHARM.

Rosalyn Randle, internationally known authority and lecturer, will give you all of these secrets in a series of free lectures. Each night a different subject.

RESERVE THESE DATES!

WEDNESDAY, THURSDAY AND FRIDAY

Feb. 9—10—11 8.00 P. M.

Francis Scott Key Hotel Ballroom

Everybody Welcome

Rosalyn Randle advertisement. *Courtesy of the* Frederick News Post.

At that point, Helen Gertrude Randle and Rosalyn Randle disappear from the newspapers. I can't think that she suddenly repented. It's more likely that she changed her name or her scam. What we do know is that her husband or the husband of another Helen Randle, Joseph LeClerc, died in 1956 and that she later married Burtis Scott Brown who died in 1964.

After a lot of research, I tracked down some of Randle's living relatives and spoke with her cousin John. He knew Helen as Gertrude and only met her a handful of times. He remembered her big car and her health center in the mountains. While the family wasn't fond of her, and she had a bad reputation with most of them, John felt that perhaps she was ahead of her time and that people didn't understand her. He is right. The ideas she touted are certainly popular and some are even respected today. If only she had promoted them honestly.

Helen Gertrude Davis Randle LeClerc Brown died on September 24 of 1980 at eighty-three years of age. Maybe that is the Helen who tried to take over Highfield; maybe not. When she was arrested in Wareham, she gave her birthdate as 1879, which would have made her over one hundred years old at the time of her death. Randle often lied about her age to promote the success of her beauty and health plans. The truth is that she was born in Greenville, South Carolina, to B.W. and Rosa Davis in 1897. Beyond that, we'll never know.

Chapter 7

STABLE THEATRE

With the death of E.H. Bristol, and after a stint as a religious retreat and hotel, Highfield and Tanglewood were transformed yet again. This time, with the help of talented visionaries and generous donors, the new endeavor would endure and become synonymous with Highfield to this day.

In 1930, according to multiple sources, Frank Beebe made a deal with a local theatre troupe, the University Players—a company with whom the likes of Henry Fonda and Jimmy Stewart began their careers on the stage at Old Silver Beach. According to George Moses, Beebe (who was then in his late seventies) did not like to go out at night. He enjoyed theater, however, very much. Therefore, he offered to take ten season subscriptions if the troupe would add a Wednesday matinee. Little did Beebe know that within a few years, the University Players would employ the services of a man who would transform Highfield and Tanglewood.

In the 1930s, Arthur J. Beckhard made a name for himself as a writer, director and producer on Broadway and in Hollywood. His career took off in 1932 when he directed and produced the Broadway hit *Another Language*, one of two Broadway plays he produced that year. That success led him to Falmouth, where he came to work with the University Players in hopes of finding his next Broadway success. At the end of his season with the Players, Beckhard directed the comedy *Goodbye Again*, in which Jimmy Stewart appeared.

After a season in Falmouth, Beckhard went on to direct more Broadway productions, including *The Comic Artist* (1933); *I Was Waiting for You* (1933); and *Wife Insurance* (1935). He also produced a number of Broadway plays: *Broomsticks, Amen!* (1934); *Picnic* (1934); *Spring in Autumn* (1935); *Suspect* (1940); *Bright Boy* (1944); *And Be My Love* (1945); and *Harvest of Years* (1948). He wrote for Hollywood films, such as *Curly Top*, starring Shirley Temple (1935); *West Point of the Air* (1935); *Sky Parade* (1936); *Border Flight* (1936); and *Pop Always Pays* (1940). He also directed *Girl on the Run* (1953).

In 1947, Beckhard returned to Falmouth, took out two mortgages and entered an agreement to buy two hundred acres of the Beebe Woods and the buildings on the property. He planned to create a summer theater as a source for his Broadway plays. He would convert the Highfield barn and stables into a theater storage space, dressing rooms and a cocktail lounge. He planned to use both Highfield and Tanglewood as hotels to house the guests that would be attending performances. He called this new venture Tanglewood Theatre and opened in the summer of 1947 with *The Hasty Heart*, a play concerning a group of soldiers at the end of World War II. Ronald Reagan starred in the 1949 film version of the play.

As good as Beckhard's productions were, he simply did not make enough money to fund his operation on the hill. With a string of frustrated creditors on his back, Beckhard needed capital to keep his theater afloat. That capital came in the form of DeWitt TerHeun.

Tanglewood Theater. *Courtesy of the* Falmouth Enterprise.

The two men met thirty years earlier in New York. Pat TerHeun explains that her father had gone to New York to "try his hand at playwriting and acting" when "he became acquainted with a young producer named Arthur Beckhard." She adds, "Never in his wildest dreams could [my father] have imagined that many, many years later he would buy a mortgage from his old friend and eventually become the surprised owner of Highfield!" Indeed the two men seemed to cross paths again and again over the years.

They met up for the second time in Greenwich, Connecticut. Beckhard was busy running a summer theater, and TerHeun was teaching at the Greenwich Country Day School. He took on the role of general business manager for Beckhard's theater.

Another decade elapsed before the two happened upon one another in California, where TerHeun worked as an organizer for the American Theater Foundation and Beckhard operated a resort theater. Yet it wasn't until TerHeun attended Beckhard's Broadway production of *Harvest of Years* in 1948 that TerHeun became involved in Highfield. He promised Beckhard that he would do what he could for the production. He kept that promise by taking over the mortgage at Tanglewood and Highfield and bought Beckhard another season in Falmouth.

Unfortunately for Beckhard, the Falmouth Playhouse was packing audiences at the same time with its star, Tallulah Bankhead. Beckhard's stint with Falmouth theater was over within a matter of weeks. After his departure in 1950, TerHeun bought Beckhard's portion of the Beebe property and instituted a corporation in order to lease the buildings.

That summer, Kingsley Perry, a member of the University Players, took over the theatre and renamed it Highfield. He spruced up the patio and bar, set up an art gallery, converted Tanglewood to dormitories and cleaned up Highfield. Most importantly, he poured the cement floor in the theatre. He began a successful season, and his assistant director took over through several successful seasons. By 1951, TerHeun was living on the hill and overseeing the Highfield Theatre operation. His daughter, Pat, describes her parents' vision:

> *Clare and my father shared a goal for Highfield which was to provide young actors, directors, and designers with an opportunity to work full-time in all aspects of theater production. They believed that originally Summer Theater was meant to be a serious training experience for young actors, and they wanted to revive that tradition. They insisted that only excellent plays be chosen every year, including three classics; Shakespeare, Shaw and Chekov or*

Ibsen were mandatory, supplemented in the 10-week season by fine modern playwrights such as Arthur Miller and Tennessee Williams. Clare was the most generous supporter, agreeing to fund any idea that came along which would improve Highfield or enhance the experience for the "theater kids." Tragically, she later had a stroke which confined her to a wheelchair and impaired her speech making it difficult for people to get to know her.

The whole family became involved in the operations at Highfield. Pat recalls her work in setting up the theater:

I made yellow and white canvas seat covers to brighten things up, painted the bar and box office, and added candles in hurricane lamps for romance. When I visited forty years later it looked almost the same, including little handwritten notes stuck up in the ladies room asking the public to respect the delicate plumbing. These looked exactly the same in exactly the same yellow bathrooms. I felt disoriented with "déjà vu."

In later years, many TerHeun family members came to visit or live up on the hill. TerHeun and his wife, Clare, were patrons of the arts and envisioned a place where students would perform multiple shows and provide exceptional summer theater. During his first season, TerHeun invited students from all over the East Coast. Totten Looney, TerHeun's niece, recalls:

The theater was such a big part of Highfield. The first play I saw there was EXCURSION. That season they also did OUR TOWN and MACBETH. Uncle Mac insisted that there was one Shakespeare play every season. I remember the witches. They wore large masks painted with florescent paint. Somehow my brother hung them on the landing of Highfield Hall and when I saw them I was scared to death. This happened after the season was over and everyone had gone home.

Pat TerHeun recalls that her nine-year-old cousins attended all of the rehearsals and became fascinated with Shakespeare. In addition to the Shakespeare rule, TerHeun had other rules for his students. He impressed upon them that they were to be respectful when they went into town—both in the way they dressed (no halters or shorts) and in the way they treated the townspeople. They were to act professionally and polite at all times.

During the first season, Tanglewood was still operating as a hotel, but by the second season, TerHeun housed students in the old Arthur Beebe home.

Their production schedule was specific and intense. Throughout, one gets a sense of TerHeun's philosophy and his love for the theater. Looney explains:

> *All students had to experience every facet of the theater from making sets, stage managing, acting, etc. The star of that week's show might be the stage manager or stage hand or painter of sets for the next week.*
>
> *Three shows were in production at once: the one on stage that week; the coming play was in final rehearsal, stage props gotten, sets finalized and on and on; the one in two weeks was in auditions for parts, staging in the rehearsal barn…Opening night was Tuesday and closing night was Saturday. Monday night's rehearsal was on the theater stage and ran all the way through without stopping, just as it would on opening night. The rehearsal Sunday night was stopped by the director or others who had to work out final problems. That rehearsal might last most of the night. Saturday night was strike night when closing show's sets were taken down and new ones put up. Another long night.*
>
> *My last year at Highfield, Uncle Mac let me have strike night parties at Highfield Hall. Wasn't much: hot dogs, chips, cookies and soft drinks. If they couldn't come to the house, I took food over to the theater for those working. I really enjoyed those parties. Uncle Mac didn't have any big serving pieces that weren't silver and that's what I used to transport food over there.*

After the first few seasons, TerHeun turned the theater over to Williams College Cross Right Stage so that he could spend more time caring for his wife, Clare. Though he was no longer specifically in charge of the productions, TerHeun still oversaw the students, their conduct and the theater schedules. He loved the theater too much to hand it over altogether. In fact, he offered his services to playhouses throughout the Cape. One of my favorite stories concerning TerHeun's generosity tells us a lot about his personality and his love for theater. Totten Looney shared the following comical stories about her uncle:

> *Uncle Mac let every theater on the Cape and maybe anywhere else in the area know that if they needed any furniture, or just anything for props, that anything in his home was available to them. And they took him up on the offer. It wasn't unusual to walk into a room and find a table, chair, sofa, lamp or something else gone. We knew we hadn't been robbed, just that someone came for props…*

One of the treasures…was a bird cage with a fake bird inside that when a key was inserted into the right place, the bird sang, flapped its wings and turned its head. Quite something to see, [but] *the key to wind it up was lost. Aunt Mickey was determined to find a replacement key…At last someone found one and the bird once again sang…No one could wind the bird up but Aunt Mickey and she only wound it up for special guests. The bird cage was in the dining room beside the bay window that overlooked the sunken garden. There was a round table in the window with all these little drawers under the top. The key was in one of these little drawers.*

So one day…I heard [Aunt Mickey] *yell "MAC! MAC!" She was definitely in distress. By now both Uncle Mac and I were in the hall. All she said was, "The table is gone!" Mac and I both gasped because that meant the key which she had spent so much time finding was gone with the table. He said that the table was at the Falmouth Playhouse. He turned to me and told me to go there right away. He would call them and tell them I was coming and to let me look in the table. I went. When I arrived, they were in rehearsal but the director stopped everything while I went on stage and found the key.*

The bird cage. *Courtesy of Elizabeth Totten Looney, from the collection of Historic Highfield, Inc.*

Falmouth Theater Guild production of *The Sound of Music*, 1960s. *Courtesy of Kathleen Byrne.*

By 1958, the Oberlin College Gilbert and Sullivan Players replaced Cross Right Stage and achieved unparalleled success that summer. They played to Falmouth audiences for a little over a decade before their director, Dr. W. Hayden Boyers, retired.

Also in the early sixties, the Falmouth Theater Guild joined Highfield. They signed a ten-year lease with TerHeun to use the theatre during the winter season.

By 1969, with the retirement of Dr. Boyers, Oberlin stopped funding its Falmouth productions and players returned to Oberlin. Two members, however, felt that summer theater should continue at Highfield, and they founded the College Light Opera Company, or CLOC.

Bob Haslun, co-founder of Highfield's College Light Opera Company (or CLOC), fell in love with theater at an early age. When he was in the fifth grade, Haslun attended a production of Gilbert and Sullivan's *Lolanthe*—a satiric comedy that includes immortal fairies and lambastes British government—and, as he recalls, "fell in love with both it and the stage."

By the time he entered prep school, Haslun knew that he wanted to study liberal arts in college. His roommates were planning on attending Oberlin College, and his guidance counselor told Haslun that Oberlin was the best liberal arts college in the country. Indeed Oberlin, located in Ohio, boasts a rich history. According to its catalogue, "It holds a distinguished place among American colleges and universities. It was the first college to grant bachelor's degrees to women in a coeducational environment and, historically, was a leader in the education of African Americans." In addition, as Haslun anticipated, Oberlin combines a topnotch liberal arts college and conservatory of music.

It was as a member of the Oberlin College Players that Haslun first came to Highfield in 1964. He continued to return to Highfield and worked as both a publicity director and general manager over the next four years. Oberlin withdrew its financial support in 1968, but in the winter of 1969, Haslun received a phone call from an old Oberlin friend, Donald Tull. Tull convinced Haslun to form a new company with him, and the College Light Opera Company was born.

From the beginning, its mission was clear, and it has remained constant over the past forty-four seasons:

> *The College Light Opera Company is an independent nonprofit educational theatre founded in 1969 and currently produced by Robert A. and Ursula R. Haslun. The Company seeks to provide fine Broadway stock musicals to summer audiences on Cape Cod, while at the same time giving young talent a chance to begin a career in music theatre. The group consists of 32 talented singers, a fine 18 piece orchestra, 12 dedicated technicians, and staff members. The Company is selected annually from applicants in colleges and universities all across the country. The members of the Company are dedicated to learning the various techniques of music theatre under the guidance of a trained professional staff.*

Of course, in the beginning, Haslun and Tull had to come up with the necessary funds to realize that mission. In his book *25 Years at Highfield: A History of the College Light Opera Company*, F. Paul Driscoll explains the company's dilemma:

> *Because time was so short, the decision was made to incorporate The College Light Opera Company as a for-profit corporation rather than wait for approval of non-profit status...At their first meeting in New Hampshire, Haslun and Tull examined their available resources, both financial and otherwise. Working capital was almost nil, but support for the new group among the network of Players alumni was encouraging. The Oberlin Players had left behind furniture, costumes, tools and music, all of which were sold to the new company for a flat fee of six hundred dollars...*

Stanley Welsh, landlord for the OberlinPlayers in their last three seasons at Highfield, agreed to grant the college Light Opera Company a lease at Oberlin's old rate for the theater and for Tanglewood.

Though Haslun and Tull continued the Gilbert and Sullivan tradition employed by Oberlin at Highfield, they also made many important changes to the theater and the schedule. As outlined in Driscoll's book, the following changes were implemented:

CLOC expanded the Highfield season from eight to nine weeks; the company as a whole was reduced in size from the complement of nearly one hundred people that Oberlin had employed at its height to a more manageable total of fifty-five; artistic Director Donald Tull believed that performers could learn as much from being in the chorus as they could from playing principal roles, and so removed Oberlin's contractual distinction between chorus and principal artists; all members of the vocal company were hired as equal members of an ensemble, and every singer would be able to audition for principal roles; CLOC signaled a bold departure from the Oberlin tradition (of the Gilbert and Sullivan canon) by introducing two bona-fide musicals…into the familiar repertory mix; and [a] *stage extension was built into the orchestra pit, increasing the available space for both sets and stage action greatly.*

Haslun feels that the old barn at Highfield is perfect for traditional summer stock. He explains:

It's a comfortable size and we don't need to mike it. There are really no major challenges. The shop is outdated and the dressing rooms are too small. There is one funny quirk—you have to stage almost all activity downstage as close to the apron as possible. The further upstage you go, the more the sound disappears into the flies.

Haslun goes on to explain another anomaly of Highfield Theater, about which he is often questioned:

You may have noticed over the years that the seating in the theatre begins with row C instead of A. We are frequently asked about this by people new to the theatre. It came that way as follows: When the theatre was built by Arthur Beckhard, it was for straight plays and rows A & B were included in the auditorium. That's also why the dressing rooms are so small. When Oberlin was invited to Highfiled, there was no room for its 26 piece orchestra and every summer the first order of business was to take out rows A & B so the orchestra could be there. At the end of the season, the last thing we did was to put rows A & B back in place. In 1966, we got permission to put in an orchestra pit. The show closed Saturday night and a local contractor came in and jack hammered the theatre floor. The company stayed up all night digging out the existing pit. A concrete person came in on Sunday and did all the mason work for the new pit. It dried all day and a carpenter came in Sunday afternoon and put in the new railings. We had a rehearsal Sunday night, and Monday we began using the new pit. When CLOC started, we used an 18 piece orchestra and so extended the stage apron several feet to its current position (hence letting us stage more downstage to help the sound problem upstage). That's the configuration that still obtains today. And that's why there are no rows A and B.

CLOC adheres to a strict summer schedule consisting of nine shows. Haslun believes that the pace is good for the company. Not only must students learn music and lines quickly, but they also have the opportunity to take part in nine shows over the course of a few months whereas most colleges produce only two shows per year. The competition is fierce, and students from all over the country apply to fill the sixty-two openings in the company (thirty-two singers, eighteen orchestra members and twelve technicians). Currently run by Haslun and his wife, Ursula, CLOC is an exceptional company now entering its forty-fourth season! In his own words, Haslun describes the success of CLOC:

CLOC at Highfield Theatre is among the very best of American summer stock companies! Located adjacent to Beebe Woods and the Cape Cod Conservatory of Music, the recently renovated Highfield Theatre is in charmingly rustic surroundings while offering the comforts of a relaxing patio and air-conditioned auditorium. Afternoons or evenings spent at Highfield Theatre are total theatrical experiences representing the finest traditions of American summer stock. The performances are thoroughly professional and CLOC is one of a very few theatre companies in the country performing with a full-size stage company and a full pit orchestra.

Little did the Beebes, who were avid theatergoers and supporters of the arts, realize that their stables would house such productions. Not only did

Highfield patio, 1960s. *Courtesy of Kathleen Byrne.*

the Beebes attend the theater, they enjoyed acting themselves. Fannie Beebe recalled a typical example in one of her journals:

> *We all went to the Thwing's Theatricals in a carriage. The plays were "Betsy Baker" and the "Little Treasure." They had been got up in such a hurry that they were almost unsuccessful…Charlie had the part of Crummy in "Betsy Baker" and Sir Charles Howard in "Little Treasure." He did not act nearly as well as usual and made several laughable blunders as "I am your wife's husband" to a man with a wife, and then to correct it, "I'm your daughter's husband" when they were a newly married couple.*

Both the Falmouth Theater Guild and CLOC have enjoyed many successful seasons at Highfield. In the end, theater survived and flourished at Highfield because of the theatergoers. Pat TerHeun emphasizes the importance of "the audiences who hung in there and encouraged the effort to present excellent theatre without stars." They and all of the players in this chapter helped pave the way for the excellent theatrical productions that we take for granted today.

Chapter 8

TerHeun's Turn

Though DeWitt TerHeun has often been described as a Texas oilman, nothing could be further from the truth. His daughter, Pat, describes her father:

> *My father was never a "Texas oil man." He was born in Austin in 1891, one of the youngest of nine children. His father was a journalist; the head of a family oriented toward literary and intellectual pursuits. All nine children graduated from college, even the girls, which was unusual at the time. The closest my father ever came to oil was when a friend of his was sent to Manchuria on a surveying mission for the Sinclair Oil Company and my father decided to go along. He loved China and chose to stay on awhile, writing for the hometown newspaper and meeting and marrying my mother. Eventually, they made their way to Paris, where in 1925 my father graduated from the Sorbonne... When we returned to "the states," my father taught at the Greenwich Country Day School until 1936, when he became headmaster of the Hammond Hall School in Los Angeles.*

When DeWitt TerHeun and his second wife, Clare, came to Highfield in 1950, they sought to bring back the splendor of the hill and create a cultural legacy. Their love and knowledge of theater brought them together, and they brought their talents and support to Highfield. The two met in 1947. Clare was the widow of Orlando F. Weber. Weber, born in Wisconsin, merged several small chemical companies into the lucrative Allied Chemical and Dye Company—a company that saw steady gains even during the Depression. Pat TerHeun describes their connection:

DeWitt TerHeun. *Courtesy of Elizabeth Totten Looney, from the collection of Historic Highfield, Inc.*

> *They had a great deal in common, particularly a love of theater and opera. Clare and my father used to go to the theater several nights a week, sitting in the second or third row and seeing their favorites over and over again. She was a wonderful stepmother to me, taking me to all her favorite places in New York and telling me interesting "rags to riches" stories.*

TerHeun's niece Elizabeth "Totten" Looney recalls visiting her Aunt Clare and Uncle Mac (as she called TerHeun) in New York at the Waldorf-Astoria. When she entered the hotel room, she was surprised to find multiple rooms within it, like a house. After visiting her uncle, she thought that all hotel rooms looked like his suite—though she said a few stays in motels cured her of that misconception quickly. She was equally enthralled with the glamour of her aunt and uncle:

> *I remember* [Uncle Mac] *as a well-dressed, proper, happy man who everyone gave deference to. For me he was something out of a movie about rich people. His wife Clare was already wheelchair bound and the only impression of her were her beautiful clothes, again like something out of a movie with bead work and lace, soft fabrics like nothing I had ever seen on a real person.*

Totten recalls that as part of her uncle's association with the Met, he acted as a judge of young opera hopefuls. One Saturday, Totten went along with her uncle. While she didn't notice any difference in the student's voices, she remembers the judges providing specific critiques for each student who auditioned. PatTerHeun explains that her father served as chairman of the Central Opera Service, which "conducted auditions leading to possible employment at the Metripolitan Opera."

When Totten and her family made their first road trip to Highfield from Texas, they met TerHeun in New York. He treated them to a Broadway production of *Oklahoma*—a very fond memory for Totten, who was a young girl at the time. The immense hotel rooms and lavish Broadway productions were only a prologue, though, to their arrival at Highfield Hall. Totten recalls, "We had no idea the wonders of Highfield until we got there. It was magical. The theater, the houses, the woods, all the actors, and the wonders of eating dinner at Highfield Hall."

When TerHeun came to Falmouth in 1950, he brought back a sense of class and importance to the hill. John Hough, son of the then editor of the *Falmouth Enterprise*, recalls his first impression of Highfield:

> *In my memory, Highfield Hall is as large and elegant as an ante-bellum southern plantation. The compound was surrounded by woods, and it felt very rustic and even remote. On a summer afternoon you might hear a clear soprano voice carrying over the stillness—an actress singing the scale, stretching her voice. I remember the sound of a banjo one afternoon, somebody picking it idly, maybe in back of Tanglewood. These sounds were lovely in the quiet of the woods.*

When TerHeun and his wife, Clare, first arrived at Highfield Hall, however, the buildings and grounds needed quite a bit of work. TerHeun's daughter saw a very different Highfield than her cousin or Mr. Hough. When she first arrived, the front hall of the mansion was packed from floor to ceiling with bedsprings. Her attempt to move them was short-lived. The scene at Tanglewood was no better, though she did find Dick Maxon "surrounded by a glamorous blonde, two hackney horses, an old coach and some miscellaneous people preparatory to becoming a parade through Falmouth." TerHeun escaped to Provincetown and did not return until the following spring.

At that time, her father began renovations of both Highfield and Tanglewood. TerHeun changed the very face of Highfield during these

Highfield, 1960s. *Courtesy of Elizabeth Totten Looney, from the collection of Historic Highfield, Inc.*

renovations—the façade I remember throughout my days growing up in Falmouth. Many viewed the new Highfield as a sort of Southern Plantation, but that was not TerHeun's intent. Pat TerHeun explains:

> *I gather the general impression is that the result of the TerHeun's reconstruction of Highfield Hall was due to some sort of obsession with the "Old South." I don't know about that, although I don't remember anyone longing for the old plantation…what I do know is this: The "setback" between the right section and the central section of the Hall was completely rotted out with water damage, and after extensive repairs it was decided to avoid a recurrence by adding a portico at the top of the building which I guess looked better with pillars. The pillars were arranged to give the illusion that the right and left wings were the same, although they were not, so maybe it was an obsession with symmetry!*

Pat enjoyed taking part in the renovations of Highfield, Tanglewood and the surrounding buildings. She recalls the experience with much detail and joy:

Rebuilding the cottage variously called "Tower House" or "John's Cottage" was the most exciting project of my life. In 1951 it was a wreck. The stairs had fallen down, the fireplace had fallen in and the walls had fallen out, and, of course, there were no bathrooms. My father wanted it completely rebuilt and ready for guests in something like eight weeks! This was obviously "impossible" but...Falmouth people seem to have a way of achieving the impossible. Half the town pitched in. All the carpenters were fantastic, furniture stores met promised delivery dates, were accurate, there were no mistakes, painters showed up on time with exactly the chosen colors. Thanks to all this amazing help, when the first guests showed up eight weeks later the house was perfect, down to can openers resting on sparkling new shelf paper in brand new drawers and flowers in every room.

Pat TerHeun goes on to say that her years at Highfield were "like a dream come true," and she cites the people who made that dream reality—the audiences at Highfield, the builders, the master craftsmen, my grandmother and the paint store owner who "opened up after hours to provide paint and rollers" and said they "couldn't eat another meal surrounded by giant red roses [the wallpaper] so we spent the night repainting the dining room at Tanglewood."

DeWitt TerHeun transformed Highfield, not for himself, but for those who could take advantage of its cultural offerings. He was truly a giving and loyal man from his earliest days. His niece Totten shared stories of her uncle's generosity with her family. As previously stated, TerHeun was one of nine children. He and his sister Mickey were raised by their oldest sister after their parents died. She had four children of her own, who became like siblings to TerHeun. She made sure that her brother and sister got a college education. TerHeun graduated from Rice University and his sister Mickey graduated from the University of Texas with a degree in library science.

TerHeun felt indebted to his older sister and invited her to live with him at Highfield. He paid all of her travel expenses and made sure he supplied her with whatever she wanted. When she commented that her Austin home would look lovely with a fireplace, he had one built. He and his wife also helped Pat, TerHeun's daughter, realize her dream of an art studio.

In the spring of 1951, Clare and my father supported my dream of having painting classes and an art gallery at Highfield. The barn became the painting studio, and a lot of white paint transformed the chicken house into a children's workshop and the stable into a gallery. Estaban Vicente, the painting teacher, later became famous as did most of the artists we showed *in the gallery. Small works by abstract expressionist painters such as Jack Twarkov, Philip Gustin, Robert Motherwell, Jackson Pollock and Willem de Kooning were priced between $350 and $700. Unfortunately for all concerned, we didn't see a single one!*

John Hough also recalls Mr. TerHeun's generosity:

I backed the stake truck into an idling car on Depot Avenue one time, the only traffic accident I've ever been in, and I had to go to Mr. TerHeun and explain it. He was sitting behind his desk and he heard me out and was as kind as he could be. Said it was an accident and I wasn't to worry about it, and that I would go on driving the truck.

TerHeun also wanted to give back to the town of Falmouth, the place to which he looked forward to retiring but never had the chance. He died in Texas in 1963. Still, the TerHeuns left a further legacy for the town by donating the land on which Falmouth Hospital now rests. In an article in the *Falmouth Enterprise*, the paper lauded TerHeun for his humble and generous nature. Though it was written some seven years before TerHeun's death, it is a telling and appropriate piece with which to conclude this chapter:

DeWitt McLaughlin TerHeun is one of our old-style newcomers. He represents what is regrettably a diminishing species. He has been among us seven years without once telling us our old ways are wrong and attempting to foist new ways upon us.

Mr. TerHeun has settled down with us to enjoy the good things which make Falmouth, and to show his appreciation of them. Of course, few newcomers have the introduction to Falmouth which has been Mr. TerHeun's good fortune. From his hilltop home he can see the beauties of the town spread out below him…His home is a stately reminder of Falmouth's rich and gracious past. History, there, clings fragrantly about him.

In the traditions of the past, Mr. TerHeun sees inspiration and hope for our achievements of the future. In this spirit he has given many acres of his old estate as the site for Falmouth's future hospital. To all the physical advantages of the site there should be added sentimental ones. The land is potentially worth a lot of money. It is healthily high. It is most centrally located. Less concretely, it dedicates a part of the property which has been a Falmouth heritage to lasting public use. It will make the hospital, upon a commanding elevation, a monument to the public spirit of the people who build it.

After the death of their parents, the TerHeun children had to decide what to do with the mansions and holdings on the hill. Because they sold the property quickly, rumors began that Dewitt TerHeun's children did not respect or care for the buildings on the hill. In actuality, they cared very much, as Pat TerHeun explains.

> *There were many family discussions about the future of Highfield. We agreed to give 22½ acres to Falmouth for the hospital, but then what? By the late fifties I was teaching in San Francisco, both my brothers lived in the West, and none of us could have supported any projects on our own so it was decided that the only fair solution was to sell the property and divide the proceeds equally. I understand that a lot of ideas were floated after that, but the spirit of Beebe Woods prevailed and now Falmouth has a theater, a school, a sport's center, a gorgeous new cultural center, and nearly 400 acres of parkland practically in the center of town. A beautiful end to one story and a marvelous beginning to another. What could be better?*

What could be better, indeed.

Chapter 9

Highfield Hall Today

To preserve the legacy of Highfield Hall for future generations, to make it a welcoming home for cultural and community life in Falmouth, and to interpret its architecture, landscape and history for residents and visitors of all ages.

—Highfield Hall Mission Statement

On a warm Cape Cod day in 1878, the first section of soil gave way, and Tanglewood—J. Arthur Beebe's magnificent summer cottage—was born. Designed by the firm of Peabody and Stearns and surrounded by the peaceful hum of Beebe Woods, the structure housed not only the family of J. Arthur Beebe but also a host of guests, students, researchers, artists, actors and musicians for nearly a century.

Almost one hundred years later—on May 20, 1977—just before the summer tourists arrived, the wrecker's ball obliterated the historic home because it had outlived its use. Some people in Falmouth, unaware of the scheduled demolition, were shocked and outraged. While they had never been particularly fond of the Beebe family, they had come to view the Beebe homes as part of their own history. Many residents had spent time on the hill and in the mansions. The homes represented a bygone era and were full of personal and historic connections.

When those of us who were too young to remember Tanglewood view pictures of the mansion, we can't help but feel an immense sadness that the home was not preserved for our generation—that someone made the decision to destroy one hundred years of history, to destroy a home worthy of preservation and use. The truth is that the house was already

Tanglewood. *Courtesy of Mike Crew.*

destroyed before the wrecker's ball arrived. By the 1970s, Tanglewood had lost the architectural features that made it a historic mansion. In a note from Maximilian Ferro, a historical expert who evaluated the home, he explained, "By the time I saw it, mantles and a host of other ornament had been plundered by break-ins, and the character destroyed by the earlier sanatorium use." Fortunately, Highfield had weathered the years far better than her sister mansion.

The Cape Cod Conservatory of Music and Art, which inherited the buildings and land from Josephine and Josiah K. Lilly III, had ordered an evaluation of both buildings. Completed by Maxamillian Ferro in 1977, the report concluded that, "Highfield Hall is a very fine mansion of the Queen Anne Revival period which still retains much of its original beauty and historical appeal." He lauded the "tall, modeled chimneys; the steep and irregular roofline; the stick work and varied textures; the hardwood floors; gilt sconces; stained glass; eight-panel doors; various mantels and overmantels; nineteenth century tiles; exquisite cornice; museum quality door trim; and the built in cupboards," among other historic design features. For a while, the conservatory gave music lessons and ran a thrift shop in the old mansion, but ultimately they could find no other viable use for the home. Highfield Hall seemed destined for the same fate as Tanglewood.

While some Falmouth residents viewed Highfield as a painful reminder of the Boston elite, they were in the minority. Thanks to the foresight and persistence of Kathy Twombly, Annie Vose and Mary Lou Smith, the people of Falmouth began to recognize the importance of protecting and preserving the historic home. The Friends of Highfield formed in 1994 to assess and repair the damage done to Highfield by vandals, animals and neglect over the years since Ferro's evaluation.

At the same time, the conservatory applied for a demolition permit. Fortunately, the demolition delay bylaw, passed during the previous spring at Falmouth Town Meeting, had been recently implemented. The bylaw provided ninety days for the Historical Commission to come up with a way to save Highfield.

According to Susan Shephard, a selfless leader in the battle to preserve Highfield, the Historical Commission and Friends of Highfield "went into overdrive" and "consulted lawyers, lobbied selectmen, circulated petitions and brought in an action team from Historic Massachusetts, Inc." As a result, they collected 5, 375 signatures, and Highfield was placed on the "ten most endangered" list.

Highfield interior. *Photo by author.*

In May 1994, Historic Highfield Incorporated was formed in the effort to further protect Highfield. Just before demolition was scheduled to begin, Falmouth selectmen voted to refer the case to the Cape Cod Commission for review. As Shephard recalls, on June 11, 1994, "Both sides presented their arguments," during what was "a long and sometimes very volatile meeting." The matter was then sent to mediation and drawn out for several years before the town voted to take Highfield by eminent domain in the spring of 2000.

During the years prior to that decision and in the years that followed, an army of local volunteers and professionals restored Highfield to its original condition. Helpers removed brush, landscaped, painted, coated wood floors, restored windows and rebuilt chimneys. They installed chandeliers and sconces. They patched ceilings and walls and stripped and recovered the roof. They installed plumbing, electrical wiring, lighting and a septic system. The list goes on and on. Susan Shephard told me, "The energy of the workers and the volunteers was amazing. We held large work parties and it was a real community effort. What you could begin to see were the bare bones of the building and that the house had barely been modified."

In addition to the work of volunteers and professionals, private donors like Jim and Ruth Clark made the substantial financial contributions necessary to complete the renovation. The people of Falmouth and the donors concerned with historic preservation made sure that Highfield did not succumb to the wrecking ball like Tanglewood.

Today, Highfield is a cultural center where residents enjoy musical concerts, art exhibits, culinary workshops, nature walks, lectures, children's programs and so much more. The mansion serves as a venue for weddings or other private affairs, houses local businesses and hosts many community events throughout the year.

When I began my research, I returned to the hill for the first time in many years. As I was used to the white plantation-style façade, I barely recognized the Highfield of my memory. In its place stood a magnificent replica of the original Beebe mansion complete with landscaping and signage.

I attended the Hounds at Highfield with my golden retriever Lucy and returned for the holiday display. I ventured through Beebe Woods and sat on the bank of the Punch Bowl. Most afternoons, I sat in the quiet of the old home and poured through the archives in what used to be Frank Beebe's bedroom.

And as I learned about the Beebes love for music, art, animals and nature, I realized that Highfield Hall today still promotes the causes and cultural

Above: Highfield Hall today. *Photo by author.*

Left: Highfield Hall. *Photo by author.*

Right: Beebe Woods. *Photo by author.*

Below: Side view of Highfield Hall. *Photo by author.*

events so dear to its original owners. I can't help but think that the Beebes would be pleased. Pat TerHeun knows that her father and stepmother would be "utterly delighted and full of admiration." She believes that the restored Highfield Hall is exactly what her parents would have wanted.

In saving Highfield, the people of Falmouth have preserved a rare example of late nineteenth century architecture. But more importantly, in saving Highfield, the people of Falmouth have created a home for themselves—one that will hopefully serve the town for many years to come.

Bibliography

Ancestry.com. U.S. City Directories, 1821–1989 (Beta) [database on-line]. Provo, UT, USA: Ancestry.com Operations, Inc., 2011.

Beebe, Charles E. *Journals*. Department of Special Collections: Stanford University, 1859.

Beebe, Frances L. *Journals*: Department of Special Collections: Stanford University, 1856.

Boston Daily Globe. "Arthur Beebe Not Drowned." July 17, 1893.

———. "Beebe Says He Is Sane, Asks Release." November 19, 1919.

———. "Defer Hearing Petition for Release of C.P. Beebe." December 2, 1919.

———. "Despondency Cause of Miss Beebe's Death." July 22, 1913.

———. "Drop Efforts for Release of Beebe: Instead, Guardianship is to be Sought in Court." December, 12, 1919.

———. "Funeral of James M. Beebe." November 13, 1875.

———. "J. Arthur Beebe a Life Member." November 3, 1894.

———. "Miss Esther Fiske's Debut." February 8, 1888

———. "Seeking Release from Asylum: Hearing December 2 in Case of Charles P. Beebe." November 21, 1919

———. "Warmed Their Home." March 1, 1892.

Catalogue of The Bolyston Medical Society. Boston: Merrymount Press, 1907.

Daily Interocean. "Drowned in Buzzard's Bay." July 17, 1893.

Driscoll, F. Paul. *25 Years at Highfield, A History of the College Light Opera Company*. Falmouth, Massachusetts: College Light Opera Company, 1993.

1870 Census. Boston War 6, Suffolk, Massachusetts; Roll: M593_643; Page: 4B; Image: 370; Family History Library Film: 552142.

1880 Census. Falmouth, Barnstable, Massachusetts; Roll: 519; Family History Film: 1254519; Page: 54A; Enumeration District: 004; Image: 0111.

Eliot, Charles William. *A Late Harvest: Miscellaneous Papers Written Between Eight and Ninety*. Boston: Atlantic Monthly, 1923.

Falmouth Enterprise. "Diet Leader's Many Claims Bring Scrutiny of Her Proofs and Past." December 10, 1936.

———. "'Eat Your Way To Health' Teacher Opens Highfield With Nine Guests." November 12, 1936.

———. "Gusts Reach 90-Mile Velocity." September 13, 1960.

Ferro, Maximilian L. "Highfield Hall: A Brief Historical Assessment." April 1977.

Fitchburg Sentinel. "Health Camp Operator Fails to Appear for Trial." November 30, 1936.

Frederick News Post. "Expert Under Arrest." December 15, 1938.

———. "Rosalyn Randle Enters Guilty Plea." November 19, 1940.

Gettysburg Times. "Doctor Asks Randle Data." December 4, 1936.

———. "'Dr. Randle' Indicted for False Pretense." December 20, 1938

———. "Mother and Son Give Testimony at Randle Trial." April 19, 1939.

———. "Mrs. H. Randle Arrested on Fraud Charge." July 27, 1933.

———. "Mrs. H. Randle to Stand Trial." February 13, 1934.

———. "Mrs. Randle Says $500 Charge Was Half of Usual Fee." April 20, 1939.

———. "Rosalyn Randle Faces 2nd Washington Trial." May 18, 1939.

———. "Says She Did Not Buy Stocks." July 28, 1933.

———. "Woman Gives Health Talks." July 10, 1943.

Hall, William S. "James Arthur Beebe." *Report: Harvard University, Class of 1869*. Cambridge, MA: Riverside Press, 1919.

Harvard College. *Records of the Class of 1883*. Cambridge, 1908.

Jones, DeWitt C. "Curtain Rising: Theater in Falmouth Over the Past Seventy Years." Woods Hole Museum.

Longfellow, Samuel, ed. *Life of Henry Wadsworth Longfellow in Three Volumes*. Boston: Houghton, Mifflin and Company, 1893.

Lumholtz, Carl. *New Trails in Mexico*. New York: Charles Scribner's Sons, 1912.

Moses, George L. *Ring Around the Punchbowl*. Taunton, MA: William S. Sullwold Publishing, Inc., 1976.

National Archives and Records Administration (NARA); Washington, D.C.; *Passport Applications, 1795–1905*; Collection Number: ARC Identifier 566612 / MLR Number A1 508; NARA Series: M1372; Roll #: 154.

National Archives and Records Administration (NARA); Washington D.C.; *Passport Applications, January 2, 1906–March 31, 1925*; Collection Number: ARC Identifier 583830 / MLR Number A1 534; NARA Series:M1490; Roll #: 198.

New Bedford Evening Standard. "The Sippican Regatta." July 17, 1893.

New England Historical and Genealogical Register. Volume 23. New England Historic Genealogical Society of Boston, 1869

New York Times. "Boston Physician A Suicide?" March 15, 1900

———. "Henry C. Bellows Drowned." July 17, 1893.

New York Tribune. "A Fatal Gale On Buzzard's Bay, Small Craft Capsize and Two Young Men Are Drowned!" July 17, 1893.

1900 Census. Boston Ward 8, Suffolk, Massachusetts; Roll: 678; Page: 10B; Enumeration District: 1263; FHL microfilm: 1240678.

1930 Census. Jacksonville, Duval, Florida; Roll: 312; Page: 12B; Enumeration District: 11; Image: 559.0; FHL microfilm: 2340047.

Rand, Edward Kennard. *Harvard College Class of 1894 Secretary's Report: Volume II.* Cambridge, 1897.

———. *Harvard College Class of 1894: Twenty-fifth Anniversary Report.* Norwood, MA: The Plimpton Press, 1919.

Redmond, Michael. "The Hammonds and Their Montecito Estate." *Santa Barbara Independent,* June 2010.

Sandusky Star Journal. "Food Expert Cooks Up $600,000 Suit." March 24, 1937.

Shepard, Susan. "Highfield Hall: Then and Now." *Spiritsail: Volume 17, Number 1.* Woods Hole, MA: Woodshole Historical Collection, 2003.

Smythe, Rev. Henry Herbert. *Letters.* Falmouth Historical Society.

Star and Sentinel. "Helen Randle, 'Sun and Diet' Woman, Sues Man for $600,000." February 27, 1937.

———."Mrs. H. Randle Arrested on Fraud Charge." July 29, 1933.

———. "Mrs. Randle is Held for Action of Grand Jury." August 5, 1933.

———. "No Decision on Mrs. Randle's Alleged Offense." January 6, 1934.

———. "7 Good Health Aids Stressed." July 15, 1933.

About the Author

Imagemakers, New Bedford, Massachusetts.

Kathleen Brunelle was born and raised on Cape Cod. She attended the University of Massachusetts–Dartmouth, where she earned bachelor's degrees in literature and writing and her master's degree in English. Her work has appeared in *Cape Cod View*, *Art Times*, *Moxie* and *The SHop*. She is the author of *Bellamy's Bride*, published by The History Press in 2010. She currently teaches English at Old Rochester Regional High School in Mattapoisett, Massachusetts. She lives with her husband, Robert, their children, Baylen and Mariel, and their golden retriever, Lucy.